HAPPY
SINGLE
MOTHER

Real advice on how to stay
sane and why things are
better than you think

HAPPY SINGLE MOTHER

SARAH THOMPSON

Thread

Published by Thread in 2022

An imprint of Storyfire Ltd.
Carmelite House
50 Victoria Embankment
London EC4Y 0DZ

www.thread-books.com

ISBN: 978-1-80314-016-2
eBook ISBN: 978-1-80314-015-5

For Stanley and Betty

Life falls apart. We try to get a grip and hold it together. And then we realise we don't want to hold it together.

Deborah Levy, *The Cost of Living*

INTRODUCTION

I am not really a single mother. My own mother reminds me of this fact as often as she can. And she is right. My children's dad is a huge part of their lives: he hasn't disappeared or left them, as so often seems to be the assumption where the exes are concerned in the single-mum narrative. He pays his maintenance, he spends time with them, he loves them. Could I write a whole book about the ways in which he doesn't always seem to get it? Yes – as most of us probably could when it comes to certain people in our lives. But he's not a wrong'un. And this book is not about the end of our relationship, or the process of our divorce, or in fact anything much to do with him at all. It's about what happened afterwards, for me, as a single mum.

But I'm not a single mum, as my mum says. And if a single mother is someone who parents all by herself, with no support or help, then it is true, I am not she. As well as their dad, I have a network of family and friends who I know I can rely on at any time to help me with the children. Occasionally I even have a boyfriend. But even when I don't, the point is we, my children and me – my little family – are very much not alone.

And yet, when my ex-husband and I announced the news of our split, I was surprised by the reactions of other people about my impending new status: Single Mother. Five years after our wedding, eleven after we had met, we were by then exhausted by the struggle. So we made a positive life choice: to extract our children from the warzone they had begun to think of as home. At least that was what I thought. But it became clear that the rest of the world wasn't quite so willing to get on board with the idea. My news seemed to bring about changes in other people that I found almost as unsettling as the divorce itself. Female friendships with other married or coupled-up mothers, ones I had considered non-negotiable, weakened without my 'other half' to complete the package of me. Their partners vanished entirely from my life now I was inappropriate company for someone else's husband. At school a teacher warned me that my children would suffer. Even my own mother, genuinely concerned, asked: 'Who will want you with two children?' To her my happiness meant being wanted, and we all know no one wants an unmarried mother, right?

It's all quite odd when you consider how boringly normal being a single parent is these days. According to the single parent charity Gingerbread, there are around two million single parents in the UK and families led by one parent make up a quarter of all families with children at home. Ninety per cent of single parents – i.e. the parent doing the majority of the parenting and with whom the children live most – are women (and are the reason why this book is called *Happy Single Mother* and not *Happy Single Parent*). How can this be? Put simply, men tend to remarry and often start new families or else live alone while co-parenting. Mothers are more likely to remain single after a marriage or relationship has ended and they still have children to look after.

That is what I am then. I am an unmarried woman who shares responsibility for her children with their father, but who looks after the children for the majority of the time. As I write this, I'm single, as in romantically unattached, but sometimes I'm not. It's hard to find the word for what I am. Single mother doesn't really cover it. I think I'd prefer independent mother, or something like that. But as a catch-all and a term that everyone else understands, it's the most efficient and familiar way of describing my situation, or predicament, depending on how you look at it.

Mine is not the only way to be a single mother. Increasingly, they are not only women who have been married or in a relationship that is now over, or who have decided to go ahead with unplanned pregnancies. Solo mums, also often referred to as single mums by choice – women who choose to conceive with donor sperm, and sometimes donor eggs as well, or to adopt by themselves – are now a significant battalion in the single mothers' army. Statistics are not easy to accurately read, because not all by-choice babies arrive via a formal clinic or agency arrangement. But the numbers are growing and look likely to continue to do so. I feel a bit envious of the 'solo mum' and 'by choice' monikers; they sound more empowered, with a hint of *Star Wars* about them. And arguably, many regular single mums are also 'by choice' in that they are the ones who have decided to go it alone after starting out in a dual-parent model. See what I mean? Hard to find the right words.

The route to single motherhood for solo mums is entirely different to that of the single mum who has separated from her partner or perhaps never been attached to him. Many of the issues single mothers by choice face are distinct, from the challenges of childcare to the way they explain their children's origins. But ultimately, to the outside world – the people who don't know the story – solo mums are regular single mothers like the rest of us, facing all the same challenges and misconceptions, joys and pains, only without the ex or the maintenance cheque.

But however we get there, whether we are single mothers post-divorce or solo mums who've conceived with a vial of sperm from a clinic, or with a friend who's happy to help, we are not a peculiarity: we are the one in four. And in fact, research by the University of Sheffield actually suggests that over a six-year period, one in three families with children will have been a single parent family at some point. Families move and blend, people split up and remarry, so that the idea of one single mother slogging it out alone forever is even more unrealistic.

Today a single mother can be a wealthy 64-year-old art gallerist like Julia Peyton-Jones, former director of the Serpentine, who in 2017 announced she had become a mother for the first time. Or she can be one of the ever-decreasing number of teenage girls who fall pregnant before they turn 18 (the UK still has one of Europe's highest teen-pregnancy rates, but despite this, teenage conception rates have fallen by over 60 per cent in the past 20 years thanks to the Teenage Pregnancy Strategy launched in 1999). She can be straight, gay or transgender, divorced, never married and, in some cases, a virgin (there is a small number of young, single women in their twenties who are choosing to have babies via IVF, either as a simple personal preference or as a result of psycho-sexual trauma, which makes sex too difficult to contemplate).

It is hard to define us. But however we arrive at our single mother status, the one thing that binds us is that we still seem to have an image problem. The words 'single mother' have connotations, even today. It's the single part. It suggests a piece is missing where a double should be. And despite centuries of progress and cultural change and emancipation, it can still be a slur. A single mother, if we are being honest, is a morally dubious woman, who is so wretched she has been abandoned or else cannot be tamed. If she doesn't work – beyond the physically and emotionally exhausting, unpaid, 365-days-a-year work of motherhood, that is – she is a drain on the state. If she does, she's a selfish, loveless woman who neglects her children and probably murders people as well. It's why you'll still read headlines and stories in all our national newspapers about single mothers instead of simply mothers, or even just women. These are just a few from a quick search for 'single mother' on the website of one national newspaper: '*Single mother slept with schoolboy 200 times*'; '*Single mother allegedly murdered son with bleach*'; '*Lords leader accused of affair with single mother*. And if she happens to enjoy a night out (i.e. not be at home with her fatherless spawn), a single mother can quite reasonably expect to be questioned by safeguarding authorities about the welfare of her children. In November 2021, the television presenter Ulrika Jonsson posted images on Instagram of her daughter's 21st birthday celebrations and told how 'two strange men' (her daughter's friends) were sleeping in her house. The post prompted her son's school to call in apparent concern for the safety of her younger child.

Switch the genders in any of these headlines and would the relationship or paternity status of the man who committed the crime even feature? Quite the opposite. In fact if a man's relationship status is mentioned at all it's rare, but to find the words 'single father' in association with anything bad or even mildly questionable is almost impossible. '*Single father is applauded for the awesome way he handled his daughter's first period*' heralded one national newspaper in 2019. In the same paper: '*Heartwarming photos show single dads and their children*' and '*Are single fathers irresistible?*' If this stuff isn't what the eye-roll emoji was made for, I don't know what is.

There is no getting around it: we single mothers occupy our very own Salem-shaped hole in society's heart. I can say these things by the way, because I know at some point I have struggled not to think them about myself.

How has this happened? The roots of the prejudice can be traced to the aptly titled Bastard Act of 1576, which gave local parishes the power to punish the mothers of children born out of wedlock with fines and imprisonment. This law formed the basis of British family law for another four centuries; it was only after the First World War, when all the men were dead, that the law finally conceded that single motherhood wasn't necessarily a deliberate lifestyle choice, or a great way to earn a living, and that single mothers should probably receive support from the state rather than being sent to the workhouse.

In 1987 the Family Law Reform Act finally gave children born outside of marriage the same legal rights as children born to married parents, ostensibly removing the ignominy around single parent families. But until then, the wholesale stigmatisation and punishment of single mothers and their children was literally enshrined in British law.

The recentness of this legal change might help in some way to understand why the stock response to news of your single parent status can still so often be one of pity with a hint of judgement, and why people will assume that your separation is a situation to be sympathised with, and worse, that your children will suffer. Or, if no father or co-parent is immediately apparent, that deciding to have a child alone is an act of desperation, a tragic last resort.

It might also explain why there's still that stale whiff of stigma in the air when we talk about single parents. Why they write articles about single mothers who receive state benefits and about whether an old woman or a virgin or a woman who used to be a man is entitled to become a mother at all. Why in culture and entertainment single mums are still so often portrayed as one-dimensional hot messes and why holidays still somehow cost the same for single parents as those travelling with partners – one of many, many hidden taxes that single mothers are forced to pay for their dissent.

And, of course, it might also explain why so many of us feel as though we have made such a monumental balls-up of our lives when we wake up to see our single parent selves staring back at us, old and unlovable, in the mirror. According to Gingerbread, single parents report almost double the rate of mental health concerns than coupled-up parents do. The realities behind those figures are not easily simplified but I think we can all agree that low self-esteem and a sense of worthlessness are the big loadstones of most mental health problems.

And yet there are so many genuinely happy aspects of being a single mother that those who judge from a distance may never understand: not only the improved relationships with our children and wider families, but the potential for new experiences and insights that the role opens up. While parenting on your own is undeniably tough, particularly if financial circumstances are gloomy, society rarely acknowledges the liberating and empowering aspects of being a single mother. Because if self-care is about setting boundaries and removing toxic people from your life, prioritising your mental health and giving yourself room for personal growth, then becoming a single parent might just be the most radical act of self-care there is. And while your social context might change, free from the mechanics of parenting as a couple, your friendships can become more varied and meaningful. You model a different, freer path for your children. We single mothers need to shout about all of that if we are ever going to tackle the stigma.

Our cultural obsession with the nuclear family – at best a Disney-esque concept, rooted in religion and fuelled by a wildly out-of-control wedding industry – makes us blind to the many possibilities and opportunities that an alternative approach can bring. In fact, all the research confirms what single parents have always known: that the way a family is put together doesn't affect the ominous-sounding 'child outcomes' (their education, mental health, career success, earnings). Two fathers, one mother, twenty siblings or none at all: none of it matters when there is love and security. It is conflict in the home – the old staying together for the kids – that is more damaging to children in the long term. That, and poverty.

With this book it's not my wish or aim to righteously prove that single motherhood is any better or worse than being part of a traditional nuclear family. I'm only saying it isn't *always* worse; you aren't automatically resigned to a life of misery as a single parent. You haven't done anything wrong because you find yourself parenting in a different structure to the one you may have anticipated, and you are categorically not a bad person for doing so, whether the choice to be a single parent was your own or one that was dumped on you from a great height. If you're a single mother, you're just a parent like every other: flawed, fantastic and financially ruined. It's my firm belief that once everyone gets on board with this concept, we can stop telling single mothers how sorry for them we all feel and get on with the job side by side and hand in hand.

This is not a guide to co-parenting, or a manual for divorce or a manifesto for singledom, although these are themes intrinsic to many of the single mums' stories in this book. Instead, I want to bust the myths and the stigma and celebrate some of the perks of parenting solo, to take a closer look at those child outcomes and highlight a few of the many positive impacts that being raised by a single parent (or two single parents, or more) can have on a child. Resilience, creativity, emotional intelligence, independence – these are the buzzwords of contemporary child development theories and nowhere are these qualities more expertly crafted than in single parent families.

This book is for every mother who is divorced or separated, has a donor-conceived child, adopts as a single parent or is simply toying with the idea of going it alone. It is for anyone who has ever felt the weight of disappointment and guilt, declared themselves a failure, been ostracised or criticised for their single parent status, who has wondered where they went wrong or why it happened to them, or who has worried about their children's 'outcomes'. This book is here to re-frame the view that being a single mother is anything other than completely fine and normal and good.

J.K. Rowling spent eight years as a single mother and wrote her bestselling series while she was parenting solo. She has said: 'I am prouder of my years as a single mother than any other part of my life.'

We should all feel proud of our time as single parents. This book is going to help us get there.

Author's note: The single mothers I have interviewed for this book come from a broad range of social backgrounds, sexual orientations and ethnicities and have all arrived at single motherhood via different routes. Some of them are single, some are cohabiting with new partners, others are in relationships but choose to live apart. Some have been married and are now divorced, some have never married but have lived with the fathers, or other mothers, of their children at some point, others have been single mums from the start. To avoid lengthy explanations and backstories, I have tended to use 'divorced' or 'separated' for relationships that have ended, regardless of whether they are legally over or had never been official marriages to begin with. It's complicated out there! But the important part of all of their stories is the part that happens when they become single mums. Names and some details have also been changed to protect their identities.

CHAPTER ONE

Such a Shame

How odd it is that we so often weep for each other's distresses,
when we shed not a tear for our own!
Anne Brontë, *The Tenant of Wildfell Hall*

I cannot pretend I was a child when I got married. I was 31, already a mother. All the signs suggested I knew what I was doing. And yet I skipped blindly down the aisle like a little girl, convinced that a vintage dress and some blousy pink roses would be enough to see me through the next 60 years of marriage. Like many of the assumptions I made about adult life, I was wrong.

Five years later, eleven after we'd met, I closed the door behind him as he left and I found myself thinking of a picture I'd seen of the actress Nicole Kidman as she left her lawyer's office on the day she divorced Tom Cruise (not, sadly, because of any physical similarities between me and Nicole). Her arms were stretched out and she was clenching her fists in something resembling joyful triumph, which made you think it was probably an image arranged by her publicist until you looked at her face and it was all contorted in a kind of spitting, angry grief that you felt sure no actress – Oscar winner or not – could possibly render.

I felt the opposing forces of devastation and relief forming a physical pain in my belly and understood that face. It was and will always be one of the most profoundly distressing experiences of my life, a sentiment I no doubt share with the 100,000 or so people who also got divorced that year, along with the untold number of cohabiting parents who also reached the painful decision that their families would fare better apart. Divorce, separation, leaving or being left: however it happens, the end of such a significant relationship is soul-bludgeoning for even the most emotionally stunted of us. They say that moving house, divorce and death are the three most traumatic life events. But anyone who has been through it knows that divorce exists in its own super league of misery. The other two are, by and large, kind of inevitable.

So when my close friends offered their sympathies I was grateful. I needed that solidarity, the gentle punch in the arm and the bottomless glass of wine they offered me. These were the shittiest of days and I allowed myself the indulgence of a fully tragic, off-the-rails experience, the dreadful, embarrassing details of which we shall never speak of again. But this was the allegiance of good friends after a break-up. It was something I had expected and felt comfortable accepting. What took me by surprise was the apparent concern, and the thinly veiled judgement, of pretty much everyone else.

To some extent, the story of my own childhood had left me ill prepared for it.

I think I was 10 years old when my sister told me that we were full sisters and not, as I had believed until then, half-sisters. I can't be certain because no one ever really talked about it after that for a very long time; it just quietly became the new truth, so the date never stuck in my mind. She said that my dad was also her dad and not, as we had both believed, my mum's first husband – the man she actually called Dad. They (our biological parents) had had an affair with each other, and she had been born while Mum was still married to her first husband and Dad to his first wife.

They did eventually both get divorced and marry each other and have me, but that wasn't until quite a few years later, and as time had passed no one had ever mentioned the bit about how she was really my dad's daughter. Even Mum's first husband didn't mention it, and he knew the truth too, apparently, although because no one had officially mentioned it, no one could be sure about that either. It had all happened in the late 1960s, long before I arrived, when love children were still frowned upon and when, if awkward things happened, everyone pretended everything was fine and went outside to mow the lawn.

It wasn't until years later that I began to think about the curiousness of this revelation and to acknowledge for the first time the quiet ripples it had pushed through my world. There had been a reshuffling of the family DNA that night but nothing much had really changed as a result of the news. It was only as I came to accept the inevitability of my own divorce, age 40, that I understood the greater truths that had also been revealed in that hushed conversation: how the constructs of traditional marriage and parenthood I thought of as solid mass had been, inadvertently, deconstructed.

So although my mum was never technically a single mother, growing up in the story of this strangely genial divorce meant that other people's reactions when I told them my husband and I were splitting up came as something of a surprise.

I live in a small town and as the weeks passed it was impossible to stay under the rocks I had so expertly positioned myself beneath at first. As I began to emerge, I faced new, unfamiliar gazes at school and at the supermarket, all the stops on the daily circuit of childcare and home management that mums with young children navigate. 'I'm so sorry to hear about you guys,' they said, next to the falafels in the chilled aisle, faces sad and crumpled, bottom lips sticking out. 'You're so brave.' They cooed, squeezing my arm like a nurse during a smear test. 'How are the kids?' they asked, as though it was any of their business, and as though simply by remaining married longer than me they had earned the right to ask. 'Much better than yours,' I muttered to myself angrily as I pushed on to the wine section. Other slightly-too-personal questions were asked too, about how I would live and how often the kids would see their father and was anyone else involved? And I couldn't help but wonder if they were asking these questions not because they really cared about my answers, but because they were scared for themselves. In my apparently sorry tale were they actually seeking reassurance that what had happened to me could never happen to them?

I understood that to an extent this was all just accepted rhetoric, the lexicon of what you say when someone gets divorced. People want to tell you they care or that they understand your pain; saying they're sorry is shorthand for that. But this was where I couldn't join the dots. It didn't always feel like genuine concern. Moreover, why would it be? These were people who I waved at in the playground, may have once sat next to at dinner. Was there something else at play here about the way people saw me now, about who I was? Because it didn't feel like concern, it felt like vultures. Vultures pretending to be budgies.

The faux-sympathy of semi-strangers was unsettling, but the responses of those closer to me felt no less bizarre. There was the good friend who surprised me by warning me to think twice before getting divorced, because if I did, I would be a '40-year-old woman on her own', as if that wasn't the whole point of the exercise. There was the teacher at school, a man I was fond of because he was always so nice about my children, and who I'd revered because he was a teacher and must therefore be wise and know everything. After he'd told me just how damaging divorce is for all children (he said all children but in that moment I knew he specifically meant mine) he told me how inconvenient it was for the school admin team when parents got divorced as they had to keep two parents informed of school news. Was divorce truly bad for all children or just the school secretary? And was the inconvenience I was causing her really something I needed to consider before I signed that decree nisi, I wondered? And had he given this same hectoring speech to my ex-husband? I suspected not. Then there was the in-law who told me solemnly that the children of separated parents never reach their full potential. And then my own mother, God bless her, asking who would want me now with two children in tow, as if finding a new husband might have been my shot at happiness, were it not for my pesky kids. Again I wondered who, if anyone, might ask my ex the same question, and drew a blank.

People said these things to me so earnestly that in those moments I felt briefly that I must surely agree with them. Because they were like me and people like me obviously saw single motherhood as a kind of victimhood and so I must think that too – yes? And why wouldn't we? The cultural references to single mothers we had all absorbed were rarely positive. As my children began to adjust to their new family arrangement I searched keenly for the books, films and television shows I could put in their way, narratives that would seem familiar or comforting to them. There were barely any, and they were still too young to appreciate *Erin Brockovich*. Apart from a picture book about some owls whose mum leaves them every night to get food, it seemed like single parent families – and in particular single mothers – were absent from children's literature and mainstream culture in general. When they did show up they were nearly always struggling social deviants defined only by their terrible alone-ness and their role as failing parent. I realised the first single mother I had ever seen on mainstream television was Mary in *EastEnders*, a drug-addicted sex worker who couldn't read.

In this context it didn't seem so unreasonable that the news that I was now an unmarried mother, untethered by man or institution, seemed to engender a sense of concern about my future and pity about what a sorry state of affairs this was.

But it was a sentiment that seemed so at odds with everything else that was playing out in the world for women in the early twenty-first century. The fight had by no means been won but we were at the height of feminism's fourth wave; people with bosoms and ovaries roamed the earth freely doing jobs, running corporations and being married or unmarried, or even married to each other, without everyone fainting about it.

Motherhood in particular had undergone a cultural transformation in the later 2010s. The blogging bubble had birthed a flurry of new and honest writing by mothers for mothers. So-called 'mummy blogs' and the books they spawned were written by women on a mission to expose the truth about motherhood: that mothers were human beings who sometimes didn't like being mothers and all its associated baking, who missed clubbing, and occasionally fantasised about having sex with the electrician. I knew this because I wrote one. Television shows and films began to depict mothers as three-dimensional, flawed characters at last. Everywhere I looked the conversation around motherhood was changing; we were quite literally coming out of the kitchen.

And yet the concept of single motherhood seemed to be locked in a time capsule, a crumb that had been missed when feminism wiped the table. Where were the single mothers in our culture who were just normal and okay? With children who were fine? The single women with children I saw all around me, at school and at work, all of them literate with no obvious heroin problem. Why were single women characterised by their career success and healthy sexual appetite (we were all still basking in the afterglow of *Sex and the City*) while single women who also happened to have children were nowhere to be seen, and if they were, were almost always pariahs? I saw Mary from *EastEnders* flash across the faces of even the most enlightened of friends, and heard those tired old tropes trotted out again and again: 'I'm so sorry.' 'It's such a shame.'

It was the tiniest shift, imperceptible to most, but I knew it had happened. I meant something different to some people now, a fact I felt uncomfortable with but couldn't yet articulate why. Was it that I felt ashamed? Yes, at times. I felt like I had tripped over on the dance floor and was face down like a starfish, while everyone else shimmied joyfully around me. Or like I was in one of those dreams where you wet yourself and everyone can see, only I was awake. I suppose I felt I had failed.

But as much as I felt the deep burn of that shame, I also felt the strong and peaceful conviction that this was the right thing to do, for all of us. And it bothered me that no one else seemed to think this. I felt shame but I also felt quite cross, because I didn't want to be felt sorry for. Why exactly was everyone feeling so sorry for me?

I began to wonder if the clue lay in the alternative response to my single motherhood. Because what is a single mother in her purest form if not a woman who is truly free? Someone who is raising children, working, surviving, unshackled by her relationship to a husband or partner. What would it mean for all of us then if, instead of feeling sorry for single mothers, we celebrated them? Maybe even aspired to be them? How would that go down with the patriarchy we were all trying to smash?

Charity case

Nothing says victim like a charity in your name so in many ways I was less than delighted to learn that in the UK single parents have one all to themselves. I came across Gingerbread during one of the first weekends that the children spent with their dad when I had made no plans to fill the unfamiliar silence they left behind them. Until then, any free time had been expertly occupied by friends, supportive sisters and my tireless mother who, despite her initial worries about my marketability post-divorce, became my closest ally. She had lost her husband – my dad – to dementia only a few months after I relinquished mine, and her house became my safe place. She saved me articles from the weekend papers, 'survival guides' written by other single mothers. I remember one who described the experience of divorce as being like leaving your husband to marry your mother. I laughed. And then I cried.

But this particular weekend I was alone at home, emptying sock drawers and re-organising store cupboards to give myself a purpose, to justify the existence of me now that I had wandered so far from the pages of my fairytale. It was still early days in the separation and the full reality of the challenges that lay ahead of me were not yet in focus; the Escher-esque mental flowcharts of income and expenditure, security and insecurity, care and damage that soon began to define my every waking thought had yet to crystallise. All I knew was that I was going to get a divorce. That was non-negotiable. The rest of the practical stuff would have to sort itself out, necessarily.

I had known, of course, that unless you were Heather Mills-McCartney the financial side of single parenthood wasn't going to be easy. I'm no mathematician, but I understood that duplicating our cost centres wasn't going to make any of us rich quick. But as I browsed the Gingerbread website – with pictures of smiling single parents pushing happy children on swings – there was something in the strapline, *helping single parents live secure, happy and fulfilling lives*, that seemed to suggest a more sinister set of problems were in store. In that simple sentence a canyon between single parents and married/cohabiting parents revealed itself, one that was far deeper and wider than finances and childcare arrangements alone. I sat in my empty family home surrounded by odd socks and out-of-date herbs, and I felt myself slip a little further through the safety net my marriage had represented. The old me, married mother, still had a foot on the right side of the net. But the new me, single mother, had fallen through the holes and was clutching at the fibres as she fell further into the abyss.

Broken parts

That in the twenty-first century being a single mother should still engender these anachronistic responses, from others and moreover from herself, seems to be a problem from the past that no one in the present has thought to fix.

Here in the present, it hardly needs pointing out that single mothers are still swimming against the muscular tide of a society built and run on patriarchal values. Times are slowly a-changing, but as any quick glance at the television newsstands or social media will testify, marriage (to a great guy) and a traditional nuclear family (with cute kids), a beautiful home (with stylish interiors) and a good body (you gotta stay young and beautiful, honey) are still pushed as the primary, and shamelessly hetero-normative, aspirations for female adults across the land.

The American feminist Kate Millett asserted in her book *Sexual Politics* that the family is the patriarchy's chief institution 'because it mirrors and reinforces patriarchal structures in society, and behaviour within the family is established and controlled by men'.[1] We have moved on since Millett wrote this in 1970 and many of the familiar dynamics have been switched up – arguably many men do not control their families any more; in fact around one in seven men now stay at home while their partner is the breadwinner (a number that has plateaued since around 2011, when presumably the novelty of being a new man wore off as men realised that going to work is way easier).

Feminism has reclaimed the entire concept of marriage in many ways, subverting patriarchal traditions with double-barrelled surnames, speeches from the bride (or brides) and dresses or *shocked-face* trouser suits that are not white.

But we also know that the *mental load* or *emotional labour* involved in running a family is still largely shouldered by women (at least in heterosexual relationships. For solo mothers by choice there is in fact no choice on this front, although solo mothers also aren't contracted to pick up another adult's dirty pants, so it's a swings and roundabouts kind of situation.) This long-standing feminist concept asserts that, even where dual-earner households are the norm, the job of remembering and executing the domestic chores necessary to keep a household running remains the woman's.

---

1   Kate Millett (2000) *Sexual Politics* (first published in 1970). Urbana and Chicago, IL: University of Illinois Press.

In her blog 'You should have asked', French comic artist Emma showed in cartoon form how even the most well-meaning husband or partner pushes the woman further into the role of family manager with statements like 'You should have asked!' and 'I would have helped!' With this attitude, women remain the people who are expected to think and feel for everyone in the nucleus: making the bread while also winning it. Academics from University College London also published a study in 2019 in the journal *Work, Employment and Society*.[2] The study found that when both partners in a heterosexual couple were in full-time employment the women, for no other reason than their gender, did an average of 16 hours of housework a week, while men, for no other reason than their gender, and even despite shared values on gender equality, did closer to six.

Throw in the fact that the British wedding industry is thriving – worth around £14.7bn a year – with women still walking down the aisle in their droves, wearing traditional dresses (average cost £1,300) and being ceremoniously given away by their fathers to men whose names they take as their own, we can safely say that marriage and its intended conclusion, the nuclear family, is still, in its essence, a patriarchal institution.

Single or unmarried mothers, by definition, have no purpose in a patriarchy. We are not meant to thrive in this situation. We are broken parts in an otherwise smooth-running engine, Atwood's handmaids, with none of the reverence about our fertility. Seen through this lens, is it any wonder our associations are so negative or that the status of single mother brings with it this arrogant assumption of personal demise and unbearable suffering?

Fortunately, it is relatively easy to clear up many of these, let's call them *misunderstandings*. To show, with some simple wiping of the lens and adjustments to our collective tinted spectacles, how

---

2 Less than 7% of couples share housework equally. www.ucl.ac.uk/news/ 2019/jul/less-7-couples-share-housework-equally

single mothers are so many things beyond the outdated stereotype: feminist freedom fighters or normal boring humans, they are parents raising children every bit as bright and capable, complicated and flawed as those who choose to do it as a couple.

The origins of stigma

Wherever there is stigma, there's likely to be someone feeling shame. Erving Goffman's *Stigma: Notes on the Management of Spoiled Identity,* published in 1963, identified in a scientific sense for the first time the idea that people feel shame when they fail to meet the standards they believe other people expect of them.[3] In a society where the loudest narrative is still *married is best* and the concept of single motherhood therefore stigmatised, it's fair to say that most single mothers are likely to be struggling with a sense of shame at some point in their life cycle, if not continually. A sense of shame has been haunting single mothers since forever.

It's not news that for centuries our religious forbears placed enormous emphasis on the bond of marriage between a man and a woman, and that those who deviated from the guidelines, issued by God himself, faced ostracisation and punishment from society, whatever their class.

Being an illegitimate child came with a number of disadvantages, mostly to do with not being acknowledged as anyone's child and not being allowed to inherit any land or money, which before there were things like jobs, tended to pose something of a basic survival problem.

But with the Bastard Act of 1576, things started to become especially bad for the mothers of illegitimate children. With this act, bastard children became the responsibility of the parish, but the mother and father were punished for their wrongdoing by being

---

3 Erving Goffman (1990) *Stigma: Notes on the Management of Spoiled Identity* (first published in 1963). London: Penguin.

charged a weekly sum for the child's care. Eventually, and presumably because female lawmakers were still fairly thin on the ground in the sixteenth century, it became the case that the mother of any child chargeable to the parish could be arrested and imprisoned until the father coughed up his dues. Mothers were punished for the father's absence and non-compliance (a system which is still in play today, with the Child Maintenance Service's Collect and Pay scheme – more on this in Chapter Two). By the early nineteenth century, all illegitimate children became the sole responsibility of their mothers until they were 16 years old. If mothers of bastard children were unable to support themselves and their children they were forced to enter the workhouse. And so the single mother as wicked wretch was with us.

Women were given the power to apply for the recovery of support costs from the father, if anyone could find him, but the responsibility still rested with her and even once recovered the costs weren't much to write home about, if indeed anyone had taught her to write: in 1872 the maximum amount was five shillings (around £1) a week. Records from the courts of Assizes (the early version of the Crown Court) for this period show that more than half of all recorded homicide victims were newborn babies. The overwhelmingly terrifying prospect of raising an illegitimate child meant many of them lost their lives before they'd even begun.

It wasn't until almost a century later, in 1974, that the Finer Report on One Parent Families finally recognised an obligation on fathers to maintain their families and identified for the first time that the problems facing many single mothers around housing, employment, income and health should probably be dealt with by the state, since single mothers seemed to already have quite a lot on their very small plates. The report proposed that mothers shouldn't need to go via the courts in order to receive child maintenance, proposals which formed the basis of the Child Support Agency – now the Child Maintenance Service that many of us know and love today.

It wasn't until later still with the Family Law Reform Act of 1987 – around the time my sister revealed to me her own blurred heritage – that illegitimate children were finally acknowledged by the law as citizens who were entitled to the same legal rights as children born within marriage (to education and health and housing and other features of civilised society), and therefore that their mothers could tick a few of the biggies off their considerable list of problems.

But as anyone who has suffered sexism or racial or homophobic abuse – all theoretically illegal – will testify, altering the law is one thing; shifting long-held public opinion is another. And even though the idea of two adults not being married (i.e. cohabiting or in a long-term relationship) is now so commonplace as to be utterly unremarkable, as is the idea of illegitimacy, pious attitudes around single motherhood still cling surprisingly fast.

On May 12, 2016, the Lyme Regis News – the small local newspaper I had ten years earlier trained as a journalist with, and had been the chief reporter of for four years – ran a piece headlined: '*Morally Behaved People Should be Top of the Housing List*'. At a recent town council meeting to discuss affordable housing, the mayor had asserted that 'more affordable housing was needed but it should go to morally behaved people rather than priority being given to single mothers and drug abusers.'

He added:

> Everybody is aware that if you get pregnant you get accom-modated, if you have drug problems you get accommodated, it is about time if you do the right thing by society you get accommodated and not ignored and left to fend for yourself.

No one with an IQ above an amoeba believes Lyme Regis Town Council is the epicentre of progressive thinking, but even taking that into account, community leaders are still out there, demonising single mothers and spouting this nonsense, their words emblazoned on billboards for everyone to ingest. Being a single mother and being a 'good' person are still somehow a binary choice in the minds of so many, particularly those in power and by proxy, the media.

Single mothers who choose to conceive using donor sperm (and sometimes eggs) attract more insidious but equally hateful headlines. These women, who have often funded their own fertility treatment and therefore can't usually be accused of falling pregnant only to get housed, are instead accused of selfishness, for having children when they are too old or depriving their child of a father. And if there is some low-key racism to enjoy, then even better. One national newspaper said on December 1st, 2021: '*Chinese mother, 53, who said ethnicity is not important after giving birth to her third child at 51 using white sperm and egg donors has welcomed her son's twin sister two YEARS later.*'

The same stories play out in mainstream culture. In the ground-breaking and very funny BBC television comedy series *Motherland*, aired in 2018–19, the single mother character, Liz, is droll and ruthless and hard not to love. But she is also unemployed and takes her children to the kebab shop for dinner; when she does cook at home she rustles up hot-dog sausages from the freezer. The joke here, apparently, is that she's a single mum so she doesn't want, or know how, to give her kids nutritious food. Even a show that did so much to dismantle stereotypes about women and motherhood couldn't quite get past the idea that single mothers are, at their core, wastrels. (Things did improve in the third series, when the posh mum who seemed to have it all was left by her husband and struggled with her own sense of shame.)

The history of single mothers' shame, the bastards and the workhouses and the unwanted babies quietly drowned – it still lingers in our fibre-broadband atmosphere. An embarrassing odour that is hard to eliminate because you can't always know where, or who, it has come from.

Alain de Botton points out, in his essay on shame, that 'few things undermine human wellbeing as much as the sickness of shame'.

Shame is different from guilt, says de Botton, in that it is not the feeling you have done something bad, but that you simply *are* bad. People who carry shame around with them believe themselves to be defective and worthless. You don't need to be a philosopher to know that those sorts of feelings don't tend to manifest well for anyone. Addiction, self-sabotage, depression and all the other things that stand in the way of a productive human life can all be linked to a personal belief in one's own pure dreadfulness.

So when a society is routinely shaming a large tranche of its mothers, the women who birth and raise its children, leading them to feel that simply by existing they are defective, things aren't going to go so well, surely? In this sense, isn't it in fact shame, not single mothers, that is the cause of all the adult suffering our culture rails against? As de Botton says, "The primary sin of those who made us feel ashamed was not so much that they spotted our flaws, it's that they forgot their own awfulness – and then had the gall to blame us for our own.[4]

The deeply held prejudices and negative public opinions that fuel single mother shame aren't something any of us can change overnight. But like any problem, the first and biggest step to solving it is admitting it exists. Or, to put it another way: when we understand and see clearly the history of our shame, we can begin to reject it.

Annoyingly, I didn't know any of this when I first became a single mother. All I knew was I'd walked into a pity-party and didn't much like the crowd. It would be some years before I could recognise the shame I was supposed to feel for what it was – a relic – and chuck it out with the rubbish. And luckily in the meantime, single motherhood began to reveal itself as something far more fun, free and empowering than everyone else seemed to think it could ever be.

4 The Problem of Shame. www.theschooloflife.com/thebookoflife/the-problem-of-shame

CHAPTER TWO

How Are the Children?

Single mothers are raising a generation of children
who are ill-raised, ignorant, aggressive and illegitimate.
Boris Johnson, *Spectator*, 1995

We had been crabbing at the harbour. I was not normally the kind of mother who did things like this; in fact, I had always taken a perverse kind of pride in being hands-off. I was a gardener, not a carpenter, whose children were free to play without my helicopter-ing omnipresence inhibiting their expression, or some other such excuse for the truth: that I preferred getting on with my own jobs to crafting wooden spoon people or making our own playdough.

But the separation had exposed me. As a working mother, living in a straitjacket of guilt was by no means a new experience. But here was fresh, next-level panic. Outwardly I talked the talk of the good, liberal parent who was like, totally cool with everything: we would share the parenting, the children could still love us both just as they always had. But inwardly, secretly, I knew I was upping my game, fluffing my feathers to make myself look and feel bigger. I read to them every night, had their friends round for sleepovers and ordered, with wild abandon, the greasy delivery pizzas I had always denied them. We got a cat.

And we went crabbing. Throwing plastic tubs into the slimy water around the boats in the bay, hoping to extract an unexpecting crustacean from its happy place, so that we could gawk at it for a while. The boy had been unusually lucky and caught an extravagant number of little crabs, 15 or 16 of them. Afterwards, as we pulled up outside the house, he rushed to undo his seatbelt. 'I can't wait to tell Da—'

My heart broke for him, as the penny dropped and the belt clunk-clicked him free. Dad wouldn't be at home.

Those were the early days, when we (the adults) still hadn't come far enough out of the fog to think beyond our own adrenaline. No routines had yet been put in place; no familiar schedules existed between us. So getting through the days and weeks – the simple tasks of arranging who would pick them up and who would do their lunches and who would watch their matches, bags left in cars and coats lost in transit – felt like mountain ranges to be climbed every day. Every text message was loaded with pathos, every wave goodbye at the door heavy-hearted and sad. When my daughter's choir performed 'All of You' by John Legend one morning, rows of happy little children belting it out off-key in the sports hall, the air putrid with the smell of PE kits and school dinners, we sat next to each other, both staring straight ahead. To have caught one another's eyes would have meant certain tears.

Going about daily life, smiling on the outside, my stomach lurched in quiet vicissitude between feelings of absolute resolve and determination that this was the right thing to do *for* them, to pure horror and fear at what it would do *to* them.

It was a dissonance made all the more complex by my children's different responses. My eldest had always disliked change of any kind. Here was a fairly fundamental and entirely unsolicited change then, for him to navigate. And certainly it was him who kicked against it most, questioning why we couldn't just get along, why Dad couldn't just be at home. It didn't make sense to him, this clever little soul. Helpless, hapless, I could only explain that one day it would make sense, and for now he'd just have to trust us. But was it the effects and implications of the change or the very concept of change itself that he was fighting? I was never sure.

His sister, younger by two years, seemed to accept the new direction life was taking her in with greater ease. Was she simply less affected by change? Was she hiding her true feelings or was her easygoing response itself a response to her brothers' objections? They so often seemed to ricochet like that, taking different directions in order to distinguish themselves from one another.

Had I ruined their young lives? Putting them through this. *How are the children?* Everyone asked it. The truth was I couldn't say anything with certainty. I could only find certainty, or something like it, in the knowledge that childhood can be as complicated and strange and beautiful and difficult for the children of parents who stay together as for those whose split. I had this certainty because mine had stayed together, and so had their dad's and so had the parents of so many of the adults I knew and liked and admired, who were just as flawed, imperfect and unhappy as everyone else.

Childhood isn't automatically better if your parents stay together. A happy childhood isn't the sole prerogative of the kids of married/ cohabiting folks.

I told myself this over and over. But it wasn't always easy to remember. I spent a lot of time online, googling myself into hysteria, about the way things were going to go for my children now that they no longer had a mum but a Single Mother. The outlook was grim.

To spare you the agony, I can report that if you are feeling guilty about becoming a single parent and want to really beat yourself up about things there are plenty of studies out there to help you get real messed up. Endless studies, all gleefully reported by the mainstream media. Reports about the effects of divorce and being raised by single parents on their poor children. Children's outcomes, their behaviour, their earnings, their relationships in later life, their life expectancy. The proportion of children raised in single parent families who go on to offend. Learning difficulties. Drugs and substance misuse. Whether they're in mainstream magazines or more serious medical journals, they all have titles like 'The psychological effects of divorce on child wellbeing and sole parent families', or 'Divorce continues to take its toll on children': the kind of titles that tell you the conclusion before you even read the article.

And of course, if you have the audacity to bring a child into the world without any perceptible father in view, then you might as well tar yourself and your children with feathers and run through the streets on fire right now. One national reported as recently as June 2021 on how a single mother had 'revealed' she felt 'empowered' after having a baby by herself at the age of 40. The headline seems unremarkable, and you wonder why they are bothering to write this story until you read in the second paragraph that the child has Down's syndrome. It is as if to say, 'That's what happens when you breed on your own, single mothers by choice.'

If you aren't convinced of their impending doom and need more persuading you might wonder what age would be least damaging for your child. If you think it's better to do it while they are younger or wait until they are older or think that eight and a half is the perfect age, then there are plenty of studies that will tell you that however old they are, that is the absolute worst age to do it to them.

Younger children will struggle with the logistics and upheaval of suddenly having two homes to live between while children in primary or grade school, who are all about right and wrong, good and bad (there is a reason children this age love superheroes), will likely blame themselves for the split. Teenagers and older children are more likely to blame you, their parents, and act out: they experience greater levels of anger and resentment; they might block you both out or favour the one they feel has been wronged. If other people are involved they will reject them. With greater independence available to them, they are more likely to disengage with family life and seek comfort in their peers and all the worrisome pastimes that teenagers tend to enjoy.

Given that so many parents opt to stay together until their children leave home (in the UK that's an average age of 24 years old; in the US it's a positively geriatric 28; in the UK the Office of National Statistics' marriage data shows divorce rates in heterosexual couples over 65 has increased by around a third in the decade between 2004 and 2014), there seems to be relatively little in the mainstream media on the adult children of divorce ('Acods' as they are known in the trade) whose parents (aka 'silver splitters') wait until they have gone then get the hell out of there.

I've always felt sorry for the Acods. They don't get to go off the rails or throw big tantrums in the supermarket when their parents split up. And they are grown up enough to understand it all.

Peter was 24 when his parents announced they were divorcing because his mother, then 46, had come out as a lesbian:

> I wasn't completely shocked because I'd always had a feeling that things could break at any moment. But I had always assumed that it would be because my dad had an affair. He was a charming man who women loved. I never entertained the idea that Mum was gay.
>
> It felt like the roots of our family had been pulled out of the ground. My dad took it especially badly and I moved in with him for a while to help him out. He was so depressed that I honestly thought I would come down to find him in a noose some mornings. I've never seen someone low like that. That was when I stopped seeing him as my dad and started seeing him as a human being who needed my help.
>
> I didn't have a problem with Mum being gay, but my brother really struggled to come to terms with it. He couldn't reconcile the fact that she had had us, her sons, and could also be a lesbian. He stopped talking to all of us for a while, just

dropped off the radar. Things are better now he has a child of his own. I think that has given him some perspective.

*

But I didn't have Acods, I had little acorns. Had I ruined their chances of becoming mighty oaks?

As a trainee journalist I learned quickly to find the fear in any story. As Annie Proulx describes in *The Shipping News*:

> We run a front-page photo of a car wreck every week, whether we have a wreck or not. That's our golden rule. No exceptions.[5]

Your story had to terrify the reader. That way they came back for more news the next day, to see if the danger had passed. This strategy speaks to the most basic of human instincts: survival.

The media reports on divorce and children raised in single parent families in a way that aims to put the heebie-jeebies up you. And despite my training, up me they went. I gulped it all down, trying to decipher the code, to determine where my children were on this new terrifying spectrum of damage I had delivered them to. Everything I read seemed like a warning, a bespoke sermon delivered directly to me, for my sins.

Certainly, there were moments when I lost my nerve, got all misty-eyed about how we could and should try again for them. Stay together for the children. As the mum of an old friend told me: in her day, you made your bed and you lay in it. My parents had always told me the story of how I wouldn't stay in bed as a child and often ended up sleeping between them, horizontally. Was I just being a naughty girl, who would not stay in her bed, and was disrupting everyone else's night in the process?

---

5 Annie Proulx (2009) *The Shipping News*. London: Fourth Estate.

Your child is unique

In her bestselling book of 2019, *Invisible Women*, Caroline Criado Perez set out to describe the gender data gap.[6] She presents to us a world of science and research and statistics in which women and their everyday lives have been, to put it simply, completely ignored. Whether it's the way car seat belts are designed (for the male torso) or the way traffic management policies fail to account for the many extra journeys mothers take every day (because they are taking children to school and doing shopping for elderly relatives before they can even think about going to work), her book is about all the things we *don't* know about the world and how we live in it, simply because we have always studied things through the lens of the masculine:

> …the male experience, the male perspective, has come to be seen as universal, while the female perspective – that of half of the global population, after all – is seen as, well, niche'.[7]

Simply because the nuclear family, led by the male, is the default and has been for so long, have we forgotten, or never learned, how to think about things in any other way? As Criado Perez puts it: 'a way of thinking that has been around for millennia, and is therefore a kind of not-thinking'.[8]

And besides, what were these studies really for? Whose bidding were they doing? When you consider that the overwhelming

---

6 Caroline Criado Perez (2019) *Invisible Women: Exposing Data Bias in a World Designed for Men.* London: Chatto and Windus, Preface page i.

7 Caroline Criado Perez (2019) *Invisible Women: Exposing Data Bias in a World Designed for Men.* London: Chatto and Windus, page 12.

8 Caroline Criado Perez (2019) *Invisible Women: Exposing Data Bias in a World Designed for Men.* London: Chatto and Windus, Preface page xii.

majority of families led by single parents are led by women, is it any wonder that all the studies and the media that reports them tell us things will turn out badly for the children of these all-girl drop-outs? In a patriarchy as mature and sophisticated as this one, what would be the value in telling us everything is going to be fine when the women are in charge?

I've got nothing against studies, they're great; but let's remember that studies – about being raised by single parents or blended families or solo mothers or whatever the circumstances under scrutiny – can only really ever be sweeping generalisations, percentages and proportions of entire genders and social demographics, huge murmurations of families made up of individual stories and personalities and feelings, flying all over the place. Every child is unique. Your child is unique.

In *How to Build a Human*, the author and scientist Emma Byrne asserts that the received wisdom of so much child-rearing is all very well but, as any decent scientist knows, you have to look at the variance and not only the mean:

> …humans are most definitely not a single, stable phenomenon. We're not trying to discover the 'true' nature of 'Baby' in the way we might determine the 'true' boiling point of water. There is no single Platonic Baby against which all others should be measured but research is often reported this way. What you'll see with your child is the variance – all the ways in which your child is unique… there is no one way to get things right.[9]

Real science, right there.

What if it is better for your child, the one in front of you and not a generic child, but yours, to raise them by yourself? Or by

9 Emma Byrne (2021) *How to Build a Human: What Science Knows about Childhood.* London: Souvenir Press, page 6.

yourselves but separately, or in pretty much any way that feels better for you and for them?

Family histories

Human beings haven't always seen the nuclear family as the best option, the deluxe package for children.

For poor women especially, the idea of providing constant care to your own children for 20 years was not even entertained until the end of the nineteenth century. For one thing, women have only regularly been making it out of childbirth alive since the discovery of antisepsis in the 1870s. But even if they got through labour mothers often died young, their children farmed out to relatives and neighbours or left to fend for themselves.

In Victorian Britain, poor children were sent away from their homes as soon as was possible. Girls went to work as domestic servants in richer households, boys went to work on farms or to live with blacksmiths and learn a trade. The idea of sending our children away to live with strangers seems odd today, but for them it was food and shelter. Safety.

A childhood spent away from your biological parents wasn't the preserve of the poor. The earliest known boarding school in the UK is King's School in Canterbury, founded in 597. Prize male students were kept apart from society at large, instructed by clergy and expected to devote themselves to religious contemplation. Staying at home, well-off girls were kept at a respectable distance from their parents in nurseries, raised by nurse-maids and nannies until they were old enough to be married off. Even children who attend regular school in America today are packed off to spend their summer holidays at 'camp', sometimes for five or six weeks at a time.

Think also of the communes – not only the hippies of the 1970s but the hundreds of 'intentional communities' that have existed since forever. Tribes, feudal vassals, religious sects. In all of these communal societies, the idea of a private family life was less important than the common experience.

In fact, the nuclear family as we think of it today, with two married parents and two happy children living at home with them both, only really came to exist in the post-war consumerist boom of the 1950s and '60s. As a race, we have distributed and raised our young in every which way since time began. And yet somehow the idea of a mother and her children, living without a man in their home, still just doesn't sit well with the world.

Grass widows

Two of the UK's largest public-sector workforces – the armed forces and the government – are built on models in which many employees, such as serving officers and members of parliament, spend time away from home. If that employee is a parent, it means long periods of time away from their family, leaving another parent in charge at home acting for all intents and purposes like a single parent. In many military families, the serving parent can be away for up to 60 per cent of the year, with little or no contact between them and their families.

A 2019 report by the Naval Families Federation found that for the children of naval families, where the father was absent for long periods of time, it was a lack of contact that was the most negative aspect of having a father in the military.[10] The report also included findings from a UK study about paternal deployment from the *British Journal of Psychiatry* in 2018, looking at fathers who had been deployed to Iraq or Afghanistan.[11] It found that the

---

10 The experience of parental absence in Royal Navy and Royal Marines families. Bridget Nicholson for The Naval Families Federation: February 2019.

11 Impact of paternal deployment to the conflicts in Iraq and Afghanistan and paternal post-traumatic stress disorder on the children of military fathers. Published online by Cambridge University Press: 18 April 2018.

fathers' deployment itself wasn't associated with any childhood emotional and behavioural difficulties, but that those difficulties were associated with 'paternal probable PTSD'. Put simply, if your dad is away on service a lot it doesn't really matter too much, but if he's not in a great way when he is around, it can cause problems for you.

Do people ask military mothers – sometimes referred to in the US as grass widows – how their children are coping while their dad is away? Of course they do. But does the wife of an army officer who is in Iraq feel there is another question lurking beneath the one being asked? Does she feel she is being shamed for having a child with someone who basically isn't there? Why should she? She is keeping the home fires burning. Where's the shame in that? They make films and documentaries about military wives and put their choirs on stage at the Albert Hall.

There are other professions – journalists, explorers, medics, musicians, rig-workers – all of which require a person, if they are a parent, to leave their children for extended periods of time, safe in the knowledge that those children are being loved and cared for by another parent or a significant attachment figure. Do the wives and girlfriends of the guitar technician or the travel writer feel judged by society at large, for choosing to have a child with someone who is absent for significant periods of time?

And there are the increasing numbers of single mothers by choice who have children by donors, or single women who adopt, where a father figure or same-sex partner has never been part of the picture. Do people ask them how their children are coping? Not really.

Ruth, who has a teenage daughter and a five-year-old son by different donors, says apart from general discussions around the topic with close friends, people don't tend to ask how her children are or how they cope with not having a dad around. 'It's always just been me and the kids, so people don't really ask. I think they assume I'm a widow.'

As a single mum who adopted her two -year-old daughter at the age of 48, Annie says her close family and friends expressed mild concern about how she would cope on her own, but never about the impact on her daughter's wellbeing, of being raised by a single mother. She says:

> My mum's first question was how was I going to afford it? But apart from that there have been no negative responses at all. Everyone has fallen for her. It's funny because I'm a single mum and an adoptive mum, but it's the adoptive bit that people seem to focus on.

That's not to say adoptive and single mothers by choice don't sometimes feel their own special kind of judgement: the idea that they are bold, brazen enough to think they can raise a child without a partner in the first place. Ruth adds:

> I've lost track of the number of times I've been told how brave I am. Which always sounds to me like what they are really saying is how audacious I am. And one particularly spikey neighbour did ask disapprovingly if my son's father even knew he had been born. You have to grow a thick skin.

The differences are subtle, but it seems that the single mother who has always been so, or whose partner is away but still married/ committed to her, is somehow more palatable – the welfare of the children much less of a concern – than the one who has had a husband or a partner and somehow managed to mislay him.

Fallen women

There is something in the marriage being over, the relationship between two parents being ended, that causes the concern. In fact it seems it is only really widows and women whose marriages or long-term relationships come to an end who inspire the heartfelt enquiry, *how are the children coping?* And the parallel with death is significant.

Because the implication of the question, when we strip it right back, lies in the assumption that things are worse now. Something is lost, someone has left and won't be back. For widows and children who have lost parents that is most probably true. But for the children of the mother whose relationship has come to an end there is not necessarily any need to make this assumption at all. In fact, there is as much reason to believe that life just got better for those children, away from the fighting and the tension that may have been their normal for months, years, leading up to their parents' split.

It is only when we play by patriarchy rules that this automatic assumption of a downturn has any currency. *How are the children (now that their father has ditched you and everyone knows you are a whore)?*

While we continue to hold the nuclear, marital family up as the ideal, other familial configurations will always seem imperfect. They'll also represent a threat to the status quo. So that when people ask how the children are, it's not really the children they are worried about at all, but the infrastructure that the success of their own lives depends on.

Nothing to see here

So, how actually are the kids? They're really doing alright, thank you very much for asking.

They don't tend to generate the kind of headlines that petrify the reader; 'Children of single mothers doing absolutely fine' just doesn't have the right ring to it. But there is research and evidence – should you need it – that can tell you that raising children as a single parent, or two, doesn't automatically mean a life of misery and crime lies ahead for them.

In 2018, the Crook Public Service Fellowship scheme at the University of Sheffield published the conclusions of a six-year research project, undertaken in conjunction with Gingerbread. The study tracked almost 30,000 children in households across the UK and found that there is in fact no evidence of:

> …negative impact of living in a single parent household on children's wellbeing in terms of their self-reported life satisfaction, quality of peer relationships, or positivity about family life. Children who are living or have lived in single parent families score as highly – or higher – against each measure of wellbeing, as those who have always lived in two parent families.[12]

Professor Nathan Hughes from the University of Sheffield, who conducted the survey, said:

> These findings have clear implications for how single parent families should be understood, valued and supported. Stereotyping single parenthood as a problem is inaccurate and immoral.
> The evidence on what affects child and family outcomes is readily available, but so often doesn't seem to shift the predetermined, negative political and media narratives about single parents and their children.

Researchers at the University of Cambridge have also explored the issue. Susan Golombok FBA is Professor of Family Research and Director of the Centre for Family Research at Cambridge. She's

---

12 Parental divorce is not uniformly disruptive to children's educational attainment. www.sheffield.ac.uk/news/nr/single-parent-families-crook-fellowship-gingerbread-1.823016

also the author of *We Are Family: What Really Matters for Parents and Children.*[13] She told me:

> There's not enough research into the positive aspects of single motherhood. It can be hard to get funding for this kind of research, and you could say it is a relatively new phenomenon, especially single mothers who are choosing to have children without fathers at all. But it is also true that most research about 'different' families has always been based on the assumption that the nuclear family is the gold standard and that any deviation from it will take a family in a negative direction. So even the positive research ends up being about the absence of negatives, as opposed to the presence of real positives.

Golombok explained that while plenty of studies show that children of single parent households are 'more likely' to experience emotional difficulties and 'less likely' to do well at school, and that many of the children of single mothers have more educational, emotional and behavioural problems than those with married/cohabiting parents:

> These are likelihoods, and there are huge variations. Many children whose parents divorce or live without fathers at home, show absolutely no negative effects. And for many of those who do, the effects improve over time, especially if divorce results in a more amicable relationship between their parents.

And, Golombok explains, showing poorer outcomes than children with two parents does not necessarily mean the absence of the father (the single motherhood) is to blame.

---

13 Susan Golombok (2020) *We Are Family: What Really Matters for Parents and Children.* London: Scribe.

In our research, we realised that the explanation (for why children of single mothers didn't do so well) seemed wrong. Growing up with a divorced single mother does not in itself appear to be harmful. Instead it's the experiences that often go with single motherhood that cause the problems. One key factor is the drop in income experienced by many mothers following divorce, which can often mean moving house or to a different place. Children have to move school or leave friends behind and that can be hard if not carefully managed.

Witnessing the conflict between their parents *before* they separate can also play a part, says Golombok. So that the damage is done by the marriage itself, long before a couple split.

Research by a US sociologist Paul Amato supports this. He looked into the long-term impact of divorce on children, comparing those of divorced parents to non-divorced parents at different ages. He found that the children born into high-conflict relationships reported greater happiness as adults if their parents had split up compared to those who had stayed together. It's a complicated concept and just not the kind of black-and-white story that the news media like to run.

But children need their father

Well, strictly speaking, no.

In 2016, Golombok and her peers at Cambridge conducted a survey to explore the emotional and developmental wellbeing of children in 51 single mother families and 52 two-parent families. The single mothers in the survey were all 'by choice' mothers who had actively decided to parent alone, whether by donor sperm or other means.

The researchers looked at positive evidence such as mother-child warmth, enjoyment of play and time spent with the child, as well as negatives like criticism and conflict. They did it through interviews as well as collaborative set tasks, like drawing a house together on an Etch-a-Sketch.

The study found no difference in parenting quality across the two groups. There was – surprise – a correlation between financial hardship and psychological difficulties for the child, but this applied equally to the single mother and two-parent families.

And in another study in 2017, researchers in Amsterdam found that children brought up by a single mother by choice do not suffer from any kind of poorer wellbeing than those brought up by two parents, and are no more likely to show signs of behavioural disorders than children raised in traditional nuclear families. The study, conducted by the University of Amsterdam, compared 69 single mothers by choice who were raising a child alone, and 59 mothers from heterosexual two-parent families. All the children were under the age of 6 and most women in the study were financially stable and educated to a degree level.

Academics found that the children of single mothers by choice benefit hugely from their mothers' social support networks, and that the idea that growing up without a father at home is not good for children, was often based on the children of divorced parents who had experienced conflict. Not on the absence of a father per se.

None of this is evidence to suggest that all fathers are unnecessary, but it is evidence to show that children raised by solo mothers are doing just fine, and can be just as happy and cared for as their dual-parented friends.

Let's talk about it

That my parents never discussed my sister's discovery with her, or me or anyone else in the world seems odd today when most of us are falling over ourselves to talk earnestly to our children about their feelings and emotions, especially when big stuff happens.

Contemporary parenting advice, of which there is no shortage, tells us to tune in to our children's emotions and try to understand how they feel: to talk so they will listen, and listen so they will talk. At school our children take classes in social and emotional learning. In 2015, Pixar's *Inside Out*, a film about the emotions inside the mind of an 11-year-old girl, became one of the highest-grossing animated films of all time.

But my parents were at the tail end of a generation that never dreamt of talking to their children with empathy about difficult experiences and uncomfortable feelings. Their own childhoods had been a time when people left babies outside in their prams all day, in itchy hats and mittens, believing the cold to be good for their health. My mum recalls being sent out in the morning with her younger brother and sister, a sugar-sandwich each in a brown paper bag, and warned not to return before dark. To the hard-working, appliance-deprived housewives of my grandmother's generation, children were a tremendous nuisance.

When it was my turn to try to talk to my children about their dad and I splitting up, I asked them how they were feeling and told them it was okay to be sad or angry. I stroked their hair and asked them again how they were feeling and told them they could talk to us both and it would be okay, and how were they feeling, until their eyes swivelled back in their sockets and they begged me to go away.

Where once adoption was kept secret even within families, adoptive parents are now encouraged to tell their children as early as possible that they are adopted and to make them feel special and celebrate it. I have witnessed this strategy in action with my friend Emma, who adopted her son Tim when he was four. She has always talked to him about being adopted and gets him together regularly with his birth brothers and sisters. They also take part in life story work, a kind of *This is Your Life* for young children who have been adopted or come through the care system that helps them understand and celebrate their own story, and how it fits in the world. He wears his adoption as a badge of honour, and rarely misses an opportunity to tell someone new his backstory. (He also sometimes tells people that the rapper Stormzy is his uncle and Taylor Swift his girlfriend.)

The advice to single mothers by choice is similar: be open about the fact there is no dad in this family as early as possible, and introduce the idea of a donor as soon as possible, ideally as soon as they are able to understand concepts such as family and parents. Being open and upfront puts honesty at the heart of your relationship and means their heritage will never come as a surprise.

When it comes to guiding our children through the change of separation or divorce, so many of us are still unsupported, or unaware of how to handle the change process. Perhaps this is because we feel ashamed – like we have failed. We don't want to acknowledge it, so we put our blinkers on and hope for the best.

But as the parent of any toddler knows, when you just come in and switch off the telly without warning them, it's not going to go down well. If you give them plenty of time to get used to the idea, if the end of telly time isn't a total shock and what is happening after the telly goes off is explained to them, and is maybe just as much fun but in a different way, then everyone is going to be a lot happier about it.

What if the shock of it – the change and its associated feelings of failure or reduced status – were the thing that really impacted children, not the fact of the divorce or the separation itself? What if the expectation, and then the redaction of, the fairytale ending was the problem?

This idea was explored in 2019 by the National Academy of Sciences in the US, with a study that focussed on the impact of parental divorce on children's education and how it varies by how likely or unlikely divorce was for those parents:

While parental divorce is generally associated with unfavorable outcomes for children, it does not follow that every divorce is equally bad for the children it affected. We find that parental divorce lowers the educational attainment of children who have a low likelihood of their parents' divorcing. For these children, divorce is an unexpected shock to an otherwise privileged childhood. However, we find no impact of parents' divorcing on the education of children who have a high likelihood of a divorce occurring. Disadvantaged children of high-risk marriages may anticipate or otherwise accommodate the dissolution of their parents' marriage. Social discourse and policy aimed at promoting marital stability among disadvantaged families, for whom unfortunate events are common, are misguided.

The circumstances are slightly different for the children of solo mums, who can experience a different kind of realisation, when they become aware that unlike lots of their peers, they don't have a father, whether he is living at home or not. Nina Barnsley, Director of the Donor Conception Network, says this can affect some children more than others.

They look around and realise that the majority of people have a dad, even if he is a bad person or dead or living far away – he is a person and usually has a face and a name. That can throw up questions like where is this man in my life? Why isn't he here? Some kids are comfortable with being different in this way, and others are very uncomfortable with it.

The Network provides support to single-mothers-by-choice with their Telling and Talking workshops and booklets, a programme that helps solo mums to talk about their child's origins and differences in a positive way, at many different stages of their development, from the early years through to the teenage years. It covers everything from body parts and vocabulary to preparing to tell them and dealing with rejection in the teenage years.

Nina Barnsley adds: 'It can be useful to have an overview of things. Getting a generalisation of the children of single-mothers-by-choice is helpful, but it doesn't tell you whether your child will be OK. It can be influenced by so many things: your circumstances and the support network you have around you, your financial situation – it is different for everyone.'

How were my children? What was the impact of the dissolution of our marriage? Had I done enough of my own telling and talking? It would be foolish of me to make grand statements here about how amazingly happy and wonderfully secure my children are. They are teenagers, so the wash is still mid-cycle and I have no idea yet what stains will be left on them in the end. All I can say is that I think the atmosphere got better at home. And the research tells us that's a good thing for them.

Almost as soon as we split, I noticed a change in the dynamics in our house. How it works in their other home I can only speculate about. You have to get good at putting their other life in a separate folder (more on this in Chapter Five). But in our home, there was, and remains, a distinct shift in the way of things.

For once in my life I find geometry comes in handy as a way of describing this. As a family of four we were a square. Two CEOs above two employees. Without their dad around so much we became a triangle. I wish I could say it is an isosceles triangle, with two equal sides and two equal angles: me at the top, overseeing the neat and tidy angles of my children. But the truth is it is more like a scalene triangle – the wild and unpredictable triangle, with no equal sides and no equal angles. Sometimes the sides are so long I can barely see the other angles. Sometimes one angle is enormous, the others tiny and sharp. Sometimes the angles are such that we are almost a line.

With the clear lines and the boxy strength of the square compromised, it very quickly became impossible to maintain the kind of us-against-them, authoritarian parenting style that we (me and their dad) had both grown up with and seemed so often to fall into. Listen to your mother. Wait until your dad gets home. Have you seen the mess in here? Good cop, bad cop. Mostly bad.

A more democratic future

My relationship with my children took on a new tone, often lighter and more frivolous. Less shouting and fewer tears, more laughter and silliness. Yes, at times inconsistent, and certainly lacking in any significant level of fear tactics or what you'd call being strict. Without another adult around, and no one to enforce the pointless new initiatives to improve behaviour (we were, thankfully, past the penny jars and naughty steps, but now there was technology and Netflix to manage), I found we became more like traders and dealers in a busy marketplace, bartering for our needs in the home. They needed more tech; I needed them to help me. I'll give you another hour on the iPad if you pick up the clothes in your bedroom. You can have another episode of *Just Add Magic* if you help me empty the dishwasher.

I found I was more inclined to let things go, to pick my battles and then possibly not even fight them. A lack of discipline typical of lazy single mothers, raising a generation of ignorant offenders? Maybe. It was partly because I was too tired, I do admit. But it was also because disharmony felt at odds with what I wanted home to be like. As the only adult in the house, I didn't want to be in a constant rage about the mess and the manners and the state of the bathroom. I liked the idea of a more democratic situation, where they at least felt like their voices were heard. Everyone needs to feel like that, even, or especially, children.

If 'trouble' happened, I had quiet discussions with them that they knew were serious because they were so quiet. The quieter I got, the more trouble they were in. I found myself talking to them like colleagues at the office – we had family meetings and wrote bullet-pointed mission-statements on the kitchen blackboard – because there was no one else around to be a parent with, to put on my parent voice for. And mostly they responded.

None of which really tells us how they are, or how they will turn out, I know. I can't tell. But who can say, with any certainty, how their children will be in the end? The problems that may or may not arise, the outcomes that may or may not be affected – are they any different, or better or worse, than those experienced in dual-parent families?

Childhood isn't automatically better if your parents stay together. A happy childhood isn't the sole prerogative of the kids of married/cohabiting folks: reminding myself of this often has been an important part of the process.

All about the teamwork

It's a cliche, but the word team is something you hear over and over again when single mothers talk about their children.

For Lara, whose twin boys she has raised on her own, the proof comes in the comments from other people:

> I think the stereotypical view of the children of single parents is these wildly out of control kids with behavioural problems and bad attitudes. But honestly my boys are so well behaved, my neighbours are obsessed with how friendly and jolly they are. They say they're not like other children!
>
> I think it's because there is no conflict, no power struggle between me and their dad in the home. What I say goes, and

I've been able to raise them in the way I want to, to be friendly and jolly.

'When I look at all the married people I know, they argue all the time. Even if it's passive-aggressive, they are at each other, in constant conflict all the time and that can't be good, can it? It must make the children feel like they are under threat. Mine don't have that, it's more of a team effort.

Victoria Benson, the CEO of the single parents' charity Gingerbread, is a single mother of six children. She says that when the first lockdown of the Covid-19 pandemic was announced, she couldn't imagine how she was going to cope, but, by the end, her family unit had become a team, the dynamics of which she knows they will always come back to in difficult times.

My children at that point ranged in age from 8 to 21. I had one who was travelling and another at university, one who was doing their GCSEs, another doing A Levels, a 12-year-old and an 8-year-old who I had to home-educate. I was also extremely busy with my job; I had a lot of work to do. Suddenly we were all in the house together, all trying to work. I felt completely overwhelmed, and there were times I felt I couldn't breathe because of the stress. The home-schooling was the hardest part; there was quite a lot of work for her to get through!

It took us a little while, but we settled into a really nice routine. The older ones would help with the home education. They would sit with her and supervise, which was lovely. We all did dog walks, together when we were allowed to. As it did for so many of us, food became a bit of a focus. We did a lot of baking, and we cooked every single day together. We had a rota, which worked out quite well in that I only had to cook twice a week. And every day we sat down to a meal together. Our meals became more and more elaborate as we tried different things. It became the focus of our day; we all sat down and ate together and we all cleared up and it was just really, really lovely. At the weekends we had big brunches and barbeques – we ate a lot of food!

It felt like we had all been on a bit of a journey together and when the lockdowns came to an end I actually felt a bit bereft. By the end of it we were all so close. When in 2021 three of them got Covid, we were pulled back into that lockdown mentality, and it took us a couple of days but we settled back into it really quickly and it was actually really nice!

A lot of the mums in the coupled families I know seemed to be full of resentment during the pandemic. The husband, or the male partner (it is always this way around), would go and lock himself in his office all day and pop out for a sandwich or go for a run, but not be involved in the home education or the menu planning or the tidying or the dog walking. That was a common theme amongst all my dual-parent friends. He got on with his job while she was doing everything else. So for me there are lots of positives about being a single mother: I can make all the decisions, there is no seething resentment and no man-child hanging around my house.

I was always conscious that I didn't have another adult in the house to talk to but I prefer it that way than to have had all the problems that so many of my married friends seemed to have to deal with.

I think the unit we became during those lockdowns will always be really strong now.

Regular families are teams, too, of course. There are undoubtedly as many stories of regular families who pull together in a crisis. It's just that no one asks them how their children are coping, or suggests their homes are broken, or expresses much concern for them at all, when they're living with a father and a mother.

I think we should recognise the teamwork that happens in single parent families as a discipline and language all of its own. The four-four-two formation might be the most common, but there are others: formations that rely on the tactical play of a lone forward and the fluent passing back and forth with the rest of their team. They all score goals and win matches; it's just that some teams play a better game when the formation speaks to their strengths.

And then there was Marcus Rashford

Football is a great provider of food for thought around single motherhood and the welfare of children raised by single mothers.

In the national lockdown of 2020, the Manchester United footballer Marcus Rashford – then aged 23 – gained a place in the nation's heart when he successfully campaigned for free school dinners to be given to children and families in need, throughout the school holidays. He also donated around £20m to food, poverty and community charities, topping the *Sunday Times* Giving List by donating more than his own personal worth. Here was a role model for the youth of today and a hero for our times. He is the son of a single mother, Melanie.

Much was made of Rashford's difficult start and the story of how, sometimes, Melanie found it difficult to provide for her son and his four siblings. In fact, the media couldn't get enough of the romantic, against-all-odds picture of a mother working two jobs to make ends meet, sometimes skipping meals herself so she could feed her boys. When England's male football team made it to the finals of the European Championships in 2021, there was further, similar coverage about the poverty-stricken childhoods of other star players, Raheem Sterling and Kalvin Phillips, both raised by 'strong' single mothers who worked multiple jobs and forwent their own meals to provide for their talented sons.

I'm the first person to put my hand up and celebrate the resilience and strength of single mothers. But where was the outrage? These mothers, British women in the twenty-first century, had to go hungry to feed their children, who also quite often had to go hungry (and who, it's also worth mentioning, as boys, were lucky enough to be able to entertain the idea of football as a career, an industry that allows them to make more money in one year than all the single mothers in the country put together. Probably.)

There was no outrage. The misty-eyed, Dickensian narrative of the wretched single mother fighting to survive is still written so deep in the collective consciousness that no one is ever horrified by it. It is my personal hope that one day Rashford and his brilliant mum, Melanie, will lead the same kind of campaign against single mother inequality and poverty that he did about school dinners. No food to feed your children is the terrible, heart-wrenching symptom, but it is certainly not the cause.

It's clear that Rashford's own childhood circumstances provided the lived-experience to fuel his passion and commitment to end child poverty. Launching his first book in 2021, he took part in an online discussion with former President of the USA, Barack Obama, who was also launching a book. Rashford talked about wanting to inspire young people to read and to believe in themselves.

Obama – arguably the most gracious leader the world has ever seen – was also raised by a single mother. Well, whaddayaknow. He talked about how women, people of colour and minority groups need to believe they deserve a seat at the table.

The idea that adversity in childhood can create extraordinary drive in adults is nothing new – we've all heard how Gordon Ramsay had a tough childhood at the hands of an abusive father, Oprah Winfrey was born to a teenage single mother and molested as a girl, and countless of the world's most successful people come from a background of hardship and struggle. But you do also wonder – at

least I do – if it is not only the adversity that creates this incredible
focus and will to do the right thing in people like Rashford and
Obama, who have used their experiences to give back to their communities. Watching this pair of caring, helpful, empathic men use
their platforms for good, to literally change the world, talking to
each other with calm consideration, I couldn't help but wonder if
an upbringing in the hands of a single mother and all that it entails
also played a part. Maybe one day, the research will prove me right.

Stitching together the patchwork week

Once we decided to split, new rows came into play about who
would have the children most and what would happen to them and
whose fault it would all be in The End. Soap-opera hangings-up of
the phone and lots of pointy shouting on the doorstep.

We were both scared. Terrified of losing the things, the people,
most precious to us. I see now that we were both only trying to
communicate our deepest, most urgent need. For reassurance and
confirmation that our children would still be ours.

And, of course, they would be. It's easy now, to say that lightly.
But at the time it was a terrifying and real prospect: the idea that
they might somehow be taken away from me, that he could fight
me for them if he really wanted to. Again I felt that conflict between
my modern, liberal values and a deep, animal sense that the children
were mine. I had grown them in my belly and no one could have
them but me. I had to bury that thought quite often.

How were we supposed to carve up our children and their lives
anyway? How should a family look, post-divorce? What was the
best configuration, the best routine? How the hell were you supposed to do this?

Like lots of people I had laughed scathingly at Gwyneth Paltrow
and Chris from Coldplay when they announced to the world that
they were uncoupling, consciously. But now that sickly promise of

an amicable, child-focussed split, all best friends and smiley smiley, seemed like a great idea. I bought the book but by five pages in I had realised we were not capable of being Gwyneth and Chris. For one thing, they were able to afford the kind of relationship counselling that could steer anyone, zen-like, through a separation. They probably had counselling every day, a therapist to talk them down from every text message. We had already bust our budget paying £45 a week for eight weeks at marriage guidance counselling, and that really hadn't gotten us anywhere, except divorced. And besides, I couldn't bring myself to read about all the things I should and shouldn't have done already to make everything okay. Life is different when you have money. In the land of money, everyone is free. I decided that celebrities and the super-rich were probably not the best place to look for inspiration on this particular topic.

But I needed at least a few instructions. I looked at the hand-drawn timetable on a sheet of A4 that I kept on the fridge, held in place by two magnets: one in the shape of a fried egg and one from a holiday in France, the top of the giant sand dune it had originally depicted now snapped off, so that only the grasses in the foreground remained and it looked like we had been on holiday to a hedge. I drew a timetable like this every term, colourful with big writing, so that everyone could see what they were doing that day or week. A horizontal line for each child, and the days of the week going down vertically. Swimming after school (take snack). Football (remember fees). Board games club at lunchtime. Tea at grandma's. Lift share with Janey. It was by no means exhaustive, and I was almost certainly the only one who ever looked at it. But it was a lifeline of sorts, a field guide to the chaos of the week with young children and two working parents.

It was before emojis, but in my mind I did the mind-blown emoji. The one where the top of the emoji person's head literally blows off due to information overload/brain malfunction. How were we supposed to divvy this all up? Was it best to make one parent responsible for everything on given days, and the other on the others? That would mean an insane amount of driving around and practically no time to work for the parent on duty, but would give the other parent a clear run, which sounded alluring. But how would you get all the necessary uniforms and lunchboxes and instruments in the right places? It seemed like a lot of hard work.

Why did we need to divvy it up at all? We could just be super-flexible and do things in a kind of cool, laid-back, as-and-when fashion. This appealed to my Chris'n'Gwyneth aspirations, but, as we were very often not speaking to each other at this point, was kind of impossible to implement. We needed boundaries. Guidelines. Rules in place. Children thrive on routine; people were always saying that. So too do separating adults.

I had read about nesting: not the kind where you buy cushions and make your house nice. Nesting in divorce-land is when the children stay in the family home and the parents move in and out (like birds) when it's their 'turn'. This seemed like the ideal solution for the children, who would not need to adjust to changes and new places, and I hope we would have done it if we had had a big enough house. But we needed another bedroom at least, ideally another wing. For us both to be taking shifts in the marital bed, in the marital bedroom, seemed kind of weird. And it would mean both of us needing to find and pay for new 'satellite' nests for the days of the week when we were not on parental duty. Nesting went into the Chris'n'Gwyneth file as something only rich people could do.

I got the calendar down off the wall. If we were going to do this 50/50, literally share the way we looked after the children straight down the line, we would need to transcend the traditional constructs of weeks and months, neither of which were conveniently composed of even units of time. You can't divide a week in two. Maybe we could do it in four-day shifts. Me Monday to Thursday, him Friday to Monday, me Tuesday to Friday, him Saturday to Tuesday... It worked but as our days changed every time it would be hard for any of us to maintain any kind of schedule or routine.

Children thrive on routine. Why exactly did people always say that? I had always rejected routines; I hated anything I had to do at the same time every week. I dropped out of book clubs and spin classes and weekly this or that, pretty much anything that made me feel that I was in a routine. *So* predictable. Snorefest. Now I found myself desperate for something to cling to, some wheels to put into a perpetual motion so that we didn't have to keep talking to each other, asking questions, arranging and rearranging, fighting and accusing. The door to an old life still ajar.

How was everyone else doing it? Online dating revealed itself to be a great window into the post-divorce worlds of other families. One of the first men I met and had a brief relationship with had not yet come to terms with his single-dad status. (He had happened upon his good lady wife in a compromising position with a neighbour and was reluctant to ever let her forget it.) We didn't last long, but that brief relationship gave me an insight into the 50/50 split arrangement. He, angry and bitter at what had been done to him, insisted he would have his three teenage children half of the time. This wasn't what she or they wanted, as his new accommodation was on the other side of the city from their family home and didn't have space for them all. His eldest, 6 ft 4-in son had to sleep on the couch. But he insisted on it; he was within his rights after all. I watched them traipsing back and forth to tick the 50/50 box and I felt a bit sorry for them. His on Sunday nights, then back to their mum's on Monday, his again on Tuesday and Wednesday before back to their mum's on Thursday, and then they alternated weekends. It was odd; while they were physically there quite often, it also seemed like they were never there. They were always coming and going. Always a bit sullen and out of place, treading water until they were on the move again.

I realised then that the 50/50 arrangement might work well for the parents but not always for the children. It was only going to be any good for us if the children could legitimately have an equal experience in both of their homes. By which I mean, they felt at home and wanted to be in both of them equally. Not that one place is a holding pen while the other place is home. And they'd need to be close by, so that the journeys between homes didn't become tiresome and miserable. If we couldn't honestly put our hands on our hearts and say that was happening, then 50/50 wasn't looking so good.

Landing on an arrangement that everyone in the equation is happy with is like trying to cook an elaborate dish full of ingredients you have never heard of and cannot easily acquire, for numerous important guests, while you are feeling quite unwell and would prefer to be lying down in the dark somewhere. Locations, jobs, preferences and needs are all mixed up and shot through with some high emotions and a dose of deliberate awkwardness from one side or both.

Chloe and her partner split up when their son Jack was six months old. His dad moved to a new town, over a hundred miles away, but was adamant that he still wanted to see Jack every other weekend. So they met on Friday evenings at a service station halfway between them.

> It was so awful. I hated leaving him like that. I usually cried all the way home. And often the journey was difficult with a young baby like that, especially on Friday nights with all the traffic.
>
> It would have been much easier for Jack and me if his dad had been closer by. It felt like it was all on me, all of the time, when Jack was small. Although now he's older and a teenager, it can be nice for us all to have the break. He gets the train to his dad's now, so it's a bit easier as well.

Jo's ex-partner moved to the opposite side of the M25 and she also found herself waiting in motorway service station car parks, to hand over her daughter every other weekend and in the holidays. 'It's fine while Georgie is young, she falls asleep on the journey, but I dread the future and how it's going to be when she wants to go to a party at the weekend or stay at a friend's and I have to tell her she has to go to her dad's, three hours away, instead. How is that going to work?'

All these different ways of doing things. It felt like a game of Child Tetris. In the end we settled on the way most people seemed to do it. A plain old one night in the week at their dad's, and alternate weekends between us. Rather than selling the house and splitting the proceeds, which would have landed us both precisely nowhere (more on this in Chapter 3), I would stay in the home with the children and we would do what the lawyers call a deferred sale (we would sell it later when the kids had finished school, or until I could buy him out, whichever came first). This way they weren't bedhopping so much. Home stayed home, for now. Their dad stayed close by. Maybe they'd see a bit less of him overall, it was true, but we'd share the holidays and he'd pick up some more of the school lifts and the incidental times, the waits in the car outside ballet or for the bus to arrive, would still be there. We'd both still go to assemblies and watch the choir singing off-key. Life would go on.

*

It would be wrong of me to pretend that living between two households does not bring its own challenges, for the children and for us parents.

When they were younger it was all the things. Books and bags and blazers and water bottles. Everything left at the wrong house or in the wrong car by children who, unsurprisingly, weren't that good at being organised. PE kit needed here or there. Thinking about the carbon footprint of our children's logistics from the primary school years makes me feel uneasy.

Now they are older they can remember their own things – mostly – but the challenges come in new waves. Teenage moods, wanting to hang out with friends instead of being with their boring parents, lifts to far-off places at a moment's notice, school books urgently needed for tomorrow in the wrong house. They are all the normal things that normal families experience, just sometimes made more complicated because there are two bases instead of one.

Mobile phones and a family group chat have made it easier; the children are part of the family discussion now and can take part in the planning and arrangement of schedules and weekends and the lifts to football. And being able to send photos and funnies, when one of us is with them or one of the children has done something, brings a new lightness to the conversations between us, the parents.

There are a growing number of apps that have been created for single parents and their families, acknowledging the huge amount of communication and planning that needs to be done to keep this kind of arrangement on the go. In the most popular of these, OurFamilyWizard, parents can trade time off, plan holidays, input schedules, pay each other and track expenses. WhatsApp seems to work best for us, but if communication is difficult between the parents or the situation complicated by long distances or other problems, I can see how an app like OurFamilyWizard would take away some of the burden. Although like all these things, people need to use them consistently in order for them to be any use.

Building resilience

It is tempting to go with the narrative that all the to-ing and fro-ing and switching and swapping is unhealthy for children, that they need stability and consistency and adults around them who are at least pretending to know what they are doing and not frantically texting WHERE ARE THEIR SHIN PADS? at each other at all hours of the day. As their teacher once kindly mansplained to me, children are like seeds: you plant them and then they just need watering and sunshine and being left to grow; they don't do so well if they get moved around every five minutes.

I could see his point. No kid needs to be brought up in a state of constant panic about the location of their shin pads. Ideally they know where the shin pads are at all times (the shin pads are a metaphor here, by the way). And yet a part of me has always wondered if this is too simplistic a prescription for the rearing of a child. Not only that, but could the need to occasionally find solutions to problems, shin pad-related and otherwise, be a good thing for children? I don't mean the kind of adversity that leaves children in single parent families going hungry – the kind the media enjoyed Dickensifying with Marcus Rashford and his teammates is not in any way a good thing – but could the switching between two parents and their households, and all of the intellectual, emotional and physical nimbleness it requires actually help them develop useful skills? Could a front-row seat to the healthy-ish functioning of a split-family teach our children a whole bunch of stuff they'd never know about if they grew up in a house where the shin pads are always in the same place? And if there is only ever one parent in their lives, do the children of solo mothers acquire skills and attributes that they might not necessarily develop in a 2.4 or a separated-parents situation?

Like swearing and street talk, the language around child development seems to change according to the phases of the moon (hands up if you've ever identified as a Tiger Mother or gone in for some RIE parenting), but for some years now we have all been told we need to be raising more resilient children. Our obese and cosseted Western children rely too heavily on being spoon-fed entertainment and need to climb more trees, play with more knives, light more fires and generally live more dangerously. Why? So that they learn to use and trust in their own instincts and decisions rather than having the world served to them on a plate. The surge in popularity of Scandinavian-style Forest Schools (some 12,000 specialist Forest School teachers now work in nurseries and primary schools around the UK) is evidence of how many parents have heard the siren call for more resilience and less CBeebies.

What's so great about resilience? Put simply, the resilient child can overcome difficult experiences and bounce back from disappointment and setbacks. They understand that things don't always go as they planned and that's okay. Instead of freaking out, they problem solve. They are empathic and able to see situations from different perspectives. And, of course, the resilient child grows into a resilient adult. Employers want resilient employees. People want resilient partners. We all want resilient kids.

So much of the research examines the 'outcomes' and the 'wellbeing' of the children of divorced, single and solo mothers, but these outcomes tend to focus on things like academic achievement, career success, health and wealth (coincidentally, the pillars of any self-respecting capitalist patriarchy). I have yet to find any studies that consider the resilience, or any other positive social or emotional attributes, developed by children who have been raised by a single mother, or between two single parent households, or by a solo mother by choice, compared to those who grow up in double parent households.

Ask any single mother though, and they'll tell you how resilient their child is.

Phillippa, a consultant oncologist who worked long hours at a London hospital, says her son Theo had to become a latch-key kid from an early age.

> He had a key and he walked home from school by himself as soon as he was able to. And he often had to heat up his own tea. I didn't have a choice; his dad had moved to France and my family weren't nearby. In the holidays he had all sorts of people looking after him! Some friends were shocked when I

told them how much he did by himself, but I always felt it gave him a sense of his own capabilities. He didn't feel neglected; there was always a lot of love and I think because I worked so much, when I was with him I was really present. I think those years of independence gave him a self-confidence and the ability to do things by himself that some of his friends just didn't have.

Kate, whose children split their time 50/50 between her and their dad, says her children have had to learn to organise themselves far more than if they had all lived in one place. 'They've had to develop an independence and resourcefulness they wouldn't have done if we had continued to live under one roof. They've learned to be a little bit more nomadic. Wherever I lay my hat, kind of thing.'

But it's not only single mothers blinded by love who will tell you their children are resilient. Joanna Fortune is a psychotherapist who specialises in the child-parent relationship, and the author of the 15-Minute Parenting series. She says:

Resilience happens when our resources to cope outweigh the stresses we are faced with. So if we want resilient children we must invest in building and strengthening their emotional resources.

You do tend to see – not always, but mostly – that the children of single parents are extremely resilient and resourceful. By which I mean they develop good independence and other resources, early on, because they have to take on a more active and responsible role at home. Things like being able to cook a basic meal, put on the dishwasher, empty the washing machine, do their homework.

In play therapy we use small-world play like doll's houses, and imaginative play like tea parties, to explore issues. I often see the children of single parents taking on a more collaborative role to functional tasks (e.g. you wash, I'll dry) with the parent in these games. Single parents give their children tasks and responsibilities earlier on. And assuming it is developmentally appropriate (we don't want pseudo-maturity, where the child is taking on a caregiver role) that is usually a good thing. It boosts their self-esteem and independence.

Children in solo-parent situations, says Fortune, have the benefit of being around a parenting style that is usually highly collaborative and task-focussed (e.g. we need to get dinner ready, versus dinner is ready), and structured but not rigid in the way some dual-parent households can be. 'They aren't exposed to the low-level bickering and strict rules that are more commonplace in dual-parent households. And they know who is available to them; the lines of power and communication are very clear.

Jo, a PA, brought up Alfie by herself for five years before Alfie's dad and his new family came back into their lives. She says the situation has helped Alfie to develop empathy and to be mindful of other people's feelings in a way he hadn't needed to be until then:

> He still protests about going to his dad's if I'm honest, but it has given him some perspective on doing things you don't always want to do, and on not hurting other people's feelings. We've had to have some pretty grown-up chats about things. He certainly knows more about some things in life because we've talked so much, one to one.

I've definitely watched my own children wrangle with feelings of guilt and a sense of duty to both of us, especially when it's time to leave one house and go to another. I remember a parting moment, very early on in our separation, when it still felt strange to be saying goodbye to them; I stood at the door waving and my daughter turned around and ran back and hugged me. With tears pouring down her face, she said, 'I don't want you to be alone.'

I didn't know whether I was more astonished by the empathy of a six-year-old or worried by the emotional strain we were putting on her by asking her to cope with this situation. All I could do, with that massive lump in my throat, was to reassure her that I actually quite enjoyed a bit of time on my own, and she would have a lovely time with Daddy until she came back home again, and it was really no different to when she went to school every day. It was one of the hardest moments of that time, and yet I'm not sure I regret that it happened. In that tiny fleeting exchange she came to understand the nature of the split, and how it was going to work out, that we both still loved and shared her and that we were both alright.

Letting them know that we – the adults – are okay seems to have been an important part of the process. As parents we worry so much about the impact on their 'outcomes' and their achievements, but I was slightly surprised by how it provoked feelings in them of protection and care towards us both. These were not feelings either of us wanted them to have to carry, and it seemed important to acknowledge them. When one of us makes a plan to do something with them, which it turns out they don't want to do, we have had to learn to let them know that we're relaxed about that, and they don't need to do everything we present them with just because we are separated. We're not offended if they don't want to come to one house or the other; they don't need to worry about us. Children who live with both parents don't necessarily have to worry about not giving them equal amounts of their time and affection. And yet, is it such a bad thing that they learn to see things from another point of view, and see two adults behaving graciously towards one another? Moreover, that they feel comfortable with short periods of separation?

Joanna Fortune says 'people permanence', the idea that you'll still be there when they come back, is an essential skill for children to develop and can inform their sense of confidence and independence as they grow up.

She says: 'Parenting solo can be an all-consuming role and yet it is essential for both you and your children to see that you have a life outside of them. When our children see us go and return it supports and strengthens their grasp on people permanence. They can accept you leaving, hold you in their mind during their absence and feel held in your mind and trust that you are returning to them. These are important skills as they get older in relationships and everyday life.'

Confronting difficult emotions is something that the children of single mothers by choice also have to do, but in a slightly different way.

Says Rowan: 'Kit is only three and has already told me she wishes she had a dad.' But instead of this being a tragic loss for Kit, Rowan feels these differences have been an opportunity to build Kit's self-esteem in a more intentional way. She says:

> When you want to live in a world that is inclusive and supports diversity, you tend to focus on difference as something that's cool, that you celebrate. As a solo mother you are more switched on to your child's development and the way your family is set up and making sure your child feels secure in that narrative. So for example at home we read picture books that are about different types of families and people, so she's actually more alert to thinking about difference, and I think in many ways has a stronger sense of her identity and self-esteem because she only has one family 'side'.

'Children need only one, available, open and securely attached caregiver,' says Fortune. 'Two is great, but not necessary. We know that children do suffer when they do not have an available caregiver. But to say that the children of single mothers don't do well or come out worse? I think it is lazy of us, as a society, to keep peddling this narrative. I certainly don't see it.'

She adds: 'Solo and single mums should not feel bad that they will need to ask their children to do some tasks for themselves or to help out a bit more or occasionally leave them with others. This is good for children and helps to build internal coping resources. Giving children opportunities to practice independence, healthy positive risk-taking (such as trying something new for themselves) and taking on developmentally appropriate responsibilities and concepts, are all good for children. It builds confidence, self-efficacy and self-esteem.'

Children of single mothers are 'ill-raised, ignorant, aggressive and illegitimate' said the UK's current prime minister (and once-divorced, twice-married father of six, or maybe seven), not so very long ago. Plenty has changed since then, but while the old broken-home BS is still coming from the top there is so much more to be done. Fortunately, the children of single mothers – free thinkers and pioneers like Marcus Rashford, Barack Obama and all the other amazing children of single mothers doing their thing literally everywhere – are turning out to be exactly the right people for the job.

Tips from the relationship support charity Relate on talking to children when you're separating

- It's important, where possible, to present a united front and tell children together so that there is one clear message coming from you both.
- It may be tempting to want to tell the children about a partner's affair, or any other perceived digressions or hurtful acts, but this knowledge won't always be helpful to the children who will have loyalties to you both and should not be asked to pick sides.
- Try to use age-appropriate language.

- Try to avoid terms like 'no longer love each other' with young children as they may worry you will 'fall out of love' with them.
- Remember it can be a loss experience for them, so be prepared to take on and deal with their emotions as well as your own.
- Be honest. There may be questions you don't know answers to, like will we move house? And where will the dog live? Say something that lets them know you don't have the answer, but that you care about the question.
- Remember to involve them but not expect them to make decisions. It's a balance between telling them 'This is what will happen' and not putting responsibility on them to make a decision such as 'Who do you want to live with?' They should be part of the process but not in charge or made to feel responsible.
- Remember to keep children central. What is best for them might mean some compromise for both parents. It is tempting to be awkward and assert your 'rights' when you are not getting on. For example, 'It's my weekend so you can't go to your cousin's birthday party.' But this usually only makes things difficult for children, who just want to go to the party.
- Remember it is an evolving process. The initial telling them is just the start and you will have many things to discuss and share with them over the coming months and years. Be prepared for questions and to listen.
- If a new partner is involved, it is important that children know that they will always share you as parents. Reassure them, with deeds and words, that a new partner is not here to take you away.
- Family counselling can be extremely helpful for families to discuss the way forward and also for couples to prepare them for telling children.

Advice on talking about solo families, from Nina Barnsley, CEO of the Donor Conception Network

There are important things to consider when deciding to parent alone, but with the right foundations it can be a very positive choice. Becoming a solo mum by choice, where there is no dad, is different from being a single mum who is separated or divorced from the father of the child. As with most things in life, there are positives and negatives in both situations. As a solo mum by choice, you won't have to negotiate with another parent, but it means all the burden of parenting and raising the child falls on just you. You won't have to include an ex's family and friends in your planning or thinking, but equally you won't have an ex's family and friends to offer support and community for your child.

Speaking to others who have been down the road already can be enormously helpful in working out if this route is right for you or not. If you don't know anyone who is a solo mum, contact the Donor Conception Network. We hold events and get-togethers where you can meet others going through the same process.

Using a UK clinic gives a certain amount of protection both for yourself and your child. Information about the donor and any half-siblings will be available; the donor will have been screened and should have had counselling to ensure they understand their role. If you are thinking of not using a clinic, make sure you have thought through the legal and practical implications of that choice.

If you are using a donor who you know or have met personally, it's a good idea to have a written agreement of each person's expectations of their role and responsibility. Try to discuss some of the more difficult situations you may find yourself in. How are you going to negotiate if circumstances change in the future or if the child expresses a different wish to whatever you and the donor have agreed?

Openness is key. There will inevitably be questions about where or who the dad is, from the child and from others, so it is helpful to think about how to answer some of those questions. Building confidence in your family story is part of getting comfortable with your decision and that confidence will be picked up on by others and your child. It can take time, including time to find the words to explain things, but there is support out there and lots of services and resources to help, so don't feel you have to do this all alone.

Plan for the practical challenges – finances, home, work, child-care, emergencies. How will you handle an emergency situation? Who will support you? Recognise that it might be tougher in some respects as a solo mum by choice rather than single mums with a partner or ex-partner.

Think about what life might look like with a baby, a toddler, a school-age child. Remember children don't stay babies forever, and you will grow older too. How old will you be when your child starts school? What does your life look like when they are in their teens? The more you can visualise these things the greater your confidence will be.

Know that there is support available. The Donor Conception Network is always here for solo mums and their families; you do not have to do this alone. One of the great joys of being part of the network is watching other families and friendships grow alongside your own.

And finally, be excited that there is this option to become a mum open to you!

CHAPTER THREE

How Can You Afford It?

There are people who have money, and people who are rich.
Coco Chanel

The first Monday of January has long been known by lawyers and marketeers as Divorce Day. This is because, legend has it, that this is the day the relationship charity Relate receives its highest volume of calls from people wishing to initiate marriage counselling. Presumably having made it through the festive period in a drunken haze, unhappy couples come round to a sober reality in January and feel they can't face another year together.

We didn't do that. We jumped before we were pushed in mid-November with just weeks to go before the holidays. Fun! So what with *everything*, I was a little behind on the Christmas shopping that year, and found myself in the supermarket at four o'clock on Christmas Eve, frantically gathering my haul. My collection of planet-killing, virgin-plastic carrier bags sat glowing radioactively at the end of the checkout, heaving with all the usual lipids, sugars and alcoholic beverages that were going to see us through the next few days. I'd be home soon and put the tree lights on, watch something good on telly with the kids, be still for a few days. I couldn't wait to get out of this place with its bright lights and ceaseless beeping. My transaction was declined.

Fuck. FUCK.

With her novelty reindeer horns flashing, the cashier picked up the bags and carried them to the customer service desk without meeting my eye once, as I tried to explain and apologise about the money magically disappearing from my account and that I hadn't realised and honestly, what a nuisance, ha ha ha. The small, town-centre supermarket was heaving with local people picking up their last bits before the big day; it seemed like everyone I knew in the world was in there to witness my festive fall from grace.

Having checked that I did in fact have zero funds in my account with which to pay for this food, which I really did need to buy as it included such Christmas essentials as the turkey and sprouts, I did the only thing I could think of doing in a crisis, what I had always done when I didn't have any money: called their dad. I asked him to come to the supermarket, pronto, otherwise Christmas would be cancelled for his children (this was before apps, when transfers took four hours and you needed that strange little calculator and your bank card to do it). I stood there, red-faced, staring into the distance while the shop jingled all the way around me. I had just asked the man I'd recently separated from to come and pay for the shopping, for a Christmas day he wasn't going to be spending with me or his children.

This was a low point.

I didn't really think about whether I could afford it: to be a single mother, how the finances were going to work. Not because I was some little rich girl who didn't have to think about money. Far from it. Ours had never been a profitable coupling. We both had pretty low-paid jobs when we met. I was a local reporter. The joke even then was that you earned more delivering the local news than you did writing it. (I hadn't yet realised there was an even bigger joke in store, that I'd earn precisely nothing when I became a mother, which conversely would be the hardest job I would ever undertake.)

So as two self-employed people, we were usually more concerned with earning money, pulling it in, than worrying about whose account it would go into or who would pay for what. We didn't do budgets and incomes and expenditures. We didn't have three months' wages saved up for emergencies. We just earned money and paid the bills and did the shopping, between us. It wasn't the kind of financial hardship many people endure – far from it. We had jobs and we ate and we had a nice warm home. But it was a kind of hand to mouth. A cycle of feast and famine that kept our heads just above water, but occasionally felt like drowning.

How were you supposed to manage money when you got married, anyway? I had never really learned. My dad gave my mum a monthly 'housekeeping' – a wad of cash in an envelope with which to buy food and keep us all fed and watered. Slave's wages. That was all I ever knew about their money. I certainly didn't know how other people did it. Although my best friend's mum had always advised us to keep a 'running away' fund, a secret stash for when the time came to leave. This seemed like a good idea, and I definitely liked the thought of having my own money. But again that uncomfortable ring of captivity. Why did my own money have to be kept a secret? And why would I need to run away? Questions that with hindsight, I wish I had asked myself more seriously.

So, when the time came, a combination of never having much money anyway and a misguided belief in my own capacity to provide meant I just kind of held my nose and hoped for the best. Apparently this is not a well-known or highly recommended financial strategy. But the idea that being a single mother was something I couldn't afford to do? Rightly or wrongly, that wasn't going to stop me.

I've always liked how Oscar Wilde put it:

> To recommend thrift to the poor is both grotesque and insulting. It is like advising a man who is starving to eat less.

Sometimes, and for some people, especially desperate people, being able to afford something just isn't as important as the having or doing of it. Besides, I hadn't married the man to improve my financial circumstances – not consciously, anyway – so why did I need to look at the price tag now that I was un-marrying him?

Maintenance: I'd heard of that. Child Maintenance Service: I had a vague idea of what that was – dads in Spidermen outfits, right? Or was that Fathers4Justice? Something to do with dads who were bad, or at least very grumpy about something, and had dragged Spiderman into it. Single mums on benefits: obviously that wasn't going to be me. Women who took their husbands to the cleaners, whatever that meant. I read a book called *Aftermath* by Rachel Cusk[14] in which she icily described the moment her solicitor told her she could be obliged to support her husband financially forever. That definitely wasn't going to be me. There was a murky, indistinct smudge of a corner of my mind where the intersection of my understanding of single parenting and money lay. I didn't think I'd be spending much time there.

I knew there were things we'd need to work out, divide up, agree on, of course. I'm no mathematician, but I knew having two family cost centres instead of one wasn't going to come cheap. But I'd work hard, and we'd survive. It was as simple as that.

A few weeks later and there I was in the supermarket on Christmas Eve, asking my newly estranged husband to come and pay for the cheese board and the hidden orange pudding that he wouldn't be enjoying with us. He did it of course, because they were his children too and hey, it was Christmas. But also because he knew, at least I hope he did, that just because he happened to be the one with the cash at that moment, it didn't mean I hadn't also earned it, being the working-mother of our children. We both worked; he just had the smackers that day. As Caroline Criado Perez says:

---

14 Rachel Cusk (2012) *Aftermath: On Marriage and Separation.* London: Faber & Faber, page 20.

> There is no such thing as a woman who doesn't work. There is only a woman who isn't paid for her work.[15]

I'm not recommending blind ignorance as a financial approach to anyone considering single parenthood, but it was a good thing I didn't think too hard about it. With hindsight it was probably a deliberate coping strategy, a flight reaction in a fight-or-flight situation. Because had I really sat down and looked at how things were going to go, how altered my circumstances would become, I may well have done a U-turn, or at least embarked on a life of crime. Because the unfortunate maths of the situation, whether you are splitting up from a marriage or partnership or going it alone from the start, are such that you probably can't afford it.

If you are divorcing or separating and one of you moves out of the family home, the big problem is that the bills in the home stay the same. The mortgage costs the same, the electricity is the same, the petrol, the food – it's all the same. Your earnings – if you have them – stay the same. If you are self-employed like me, they may actually shrink as you struggle to balance the need to earn while also needing to be more present for the children. Now no one else can pop out to pick them up or get some milk or in fact do anything helpful around here, except you. Everything is exactly the same, only now there is a gaping hole where the other adult's wages used to be and you are even more stretched, physically and mentally, than you were before. You are doing far, far more for much, much less.

Yes, there are savings, ways to offset this new, worrying deficit in your domestic purchase ledger. You do get a single-person discount on the council tax, but (and depending on your local authority) it's a 25 per cent discount, not half. So as an individual who was previously paying 50 per cent of this tax along with your spouse,

---

15 Caroline Criado Perez (2019) *Invisible Women: Exposing Data Bias in a World Designed for Men.* London: Chatto and Windus, page 70.

you are technically paying more council tax (75 per cent) than you did before. You are paying a premium because you are single. (If you are a woman and feeling particularly feministy, which if you're not already I'm willing to bet you will be soon, you might also call this a massive tax on your gender.) There might be a small dent in the food bills with one less adult mouth to feed, but that is easily made up for by the take-aways and the new pets you buy to assuage your guilt for being the worst mother ever. If your children are teenagers, they may also begin to digest the actual cupboards and other pieces of furniture in their never-ending quest to quell their hunger.

So you might reluctantly think of selling the family home and imagine splitting the spoils with your ex and cosying yourself and the kids up in a cute garden flat somewhere. But assuming you are mortgaged to the eyeballs and living in a family home that only just about fits you all and the hamsters (who frankly get more square metres and floor-to-ceiling windows), you are likely to find that one into two does not easily go. You might find, as we did, that selling the house would only leave both parents in a situation where neither of you can afford somewhere suitable for your family.

Even if you somehow find two perfect homes with all the necessary rooms, close to each other and their schools and all the other boxes you need to tick, you are likely to find getting a mortgage something of an ultra-marathon you haven't trained for. Mortgage lenders don't tend to fall over themselves to invest in single parents, especially mothers, who usually have the chicks in the nest more often, demanding all that food and warmth. Why? Because in the holy mortgage trinity of income, outgoings and affordability, your average single mother scores low on all three. Income is lower because she's a woman and more likely to work part time, outgoings are higher because she has the children at home with her more and all their associated bills, and so the affordability for her of any large, expensive loan – say for example, a mortgage – is up the spout.

Renting is no less inaccessible to the newly single mother, who, if she can just about afford the extortionate price of renting a home big enough for her family every month (because no one is offering a discount to single mothers, believe me), will also need to find an extortionate deposit upfront and all the various other extortionate moving-in fees demanded by evil buy-to-let landlords. Yes, if your income is below a certain threshold there is housing benefit, which can be used in the private sector as well as with social housing, and some councils provide help with the upfront costs of moving in (known as a discretionary housing payment and/or tenancy support), but these are by no means automatic and will involve much hoop-jumping and shape-shifting and long, protracted administrational nightmares, which you may not be up for at this point. (Aptly named charities such as Crisis and Shelter can help you find the schemes that are available in your area.) This of course assumes you have found the one landlord in the land who accepts housing benefit – and hamsters.

Plenty of single dads don't have it any easier, by the way, and, as the ones who are most often faced with the job of moving out of the family home, are often forced to find new and unusual ways of circumventing the financial challenges of splitting up.

In London, there's a growing flotilla of divorced fathers who are making their home on canal barges. Cheaper mortgages and very low running costs make it one of the most affordable housing options in the capital. Pamela Smith, chair of the National Bargee and Traveller Association, a group representing the interests of people who live aboard barges in the UK, said:

> What we have noticed for at least 10 years and probably a lot longer is that there is a significant number of divorced men moving onto boats when the family home is sold or their share bought out by their ex. They don't have enough money from the sale of the family home to buy another house. Some of these men have non-resident children staying with them for part of the time.

In fact I have only met one dad – a doctor – who had the funds to buy himself a house when he left the family home. Ironically, and very sadly, he was also the one who had the most distant and unhappy relationship with his son. I met a dad who slept on the sofa when his teenage daughters visited once a week, so they could have his room. I met another who lived in a campervan and took his kids camping on the weekends he had them: summer and winter. Another moved north and met his teenage sons in different Airbnbs in the Midlands every fortnight, this being cheaper than buying or renting in the south.

All these ingenious ways around the system are great, but you can't help thinking they leave little room for the children to find a space that is theirs. The children become houseguests: there for sleepovers, not at their home. Again, it's not the poverty and over-crowding that many families endure, but if the change in lifestyle is sufficiently shocking to them, you wonder what the longer-term impact of half a childhood spent feeling out of place might be.

For some couples, this kind of advanced mathematical physics can be too much to bear, and they decide to stay living together under one roof, because at the end of the day they have no choice. At least they don't have to go through all the upheaval of moving, the kids get to keep their bedrooms and the dull and emotionally draining process of unpicking their lives can stay at the bottom of the to-do list for another miserable, loveless decade.

This way of living-together-apart is now so common that it is even being recognised by the banks and mortgage lenders, some of whom now offer separation agreements specifically for couples who plan to continue living together. The Co-Op Legal offers one that promises to help you work out the bills 'until you vacate your home'.

(In the US, this arrangement is sometimes known as a Parenting Marriage, which sounds much nicer but also a bit like a Steve Martin romcom, where they split up but stay living together, and, via a series of hilarious 'coincidences' secretly arranged by their children, realise how much they love each other and get back together in the end.)

For Ashe there was simply no other way of doing it:

We are both directors in a business we founded together. Being a director sounds very grand but in reality doesn't mean I get a huge salary at all. It also meant I couldn't claim any kind of tax credits or housing support when we split up, so I basically wouldn't have had an income and couldn't afford to live anywhere else. I looked at other jobs, ways around it, but nothing was viable. So I stayed put and so did their dad.

For a long time it was really horrible. I felt so trapped. There were days I wanted to lock myself in a cupboard and not come out. I can remember having a panic attack in Marks & Spencer. I couldn't decide what flavour crisps to buy, and it just sent me over the edge. The whole thing really opened my eyes to the way things work, and why when people tell women in abusive relationships to leave, it's just not that simple. We'd never even had a joint bank account as a married couple, we'd always just shared the costs, but now I felt tied permanently to the family home.

So we decided to make a go of living together as a separated couple. He stayed upstairs with the en suite and I moved into the spare bedroom, on the same floor as the kids. Having our own bathrooms helps. We've worked really hard, and I'm proud of how we've made a go of it. We're still legally married; we didn't want to spend the money on getting divorced. But other people's attitudes have been hard to cope with at times. There isn't a word for what Rob and I are. People don't know if they can invite us for dinner, whose side they are supposed to be on. I think we would both have better social lives if we didn't live together like this, but the flip side is neither of us is missing out on family life with the children.

In some ways it's a clever calling of the patriarchal bluff. A twisted can't-beat-em-join-em approach that saves everyone the stress and indignity of losing their home and keeps them both in with a chance of one day seeing a return on the many thousands of pounds they may have chucked at it over the years. But it seems to leave little room for a new life. Like being locked in the cinema at the end of the film, with the last song playing on repeat and only popcorn off the floor to eat, until your children leave home, and someone finally lets you out into the light.

Best of luck to the good folk who can pull this off. There's a place in heaven waiting for you. We had already spent months living quite separately on the same turf and concluded this was not a vision of a future that either of us could claim to want. That approach was never going to work for us. Nope.

Solo mothers by choice face a different set of financial challenges. It's widely accepted that this demographic is more affluent and financially independent than single mothers who come to their status via happy accident or separation. For one thing, if they are heterosexual and able-bodied and single, they are unlikely to qualify for NHS funding, which is reserved for the couples who have been trying for a long time and/or minority groups. (No one begrudges these people the funding they deserve, but I can't be the only person who thinks it's a bit sinister when they won't also fund straight single women – is the thinking that they could just marry a man and stop wasting the fertility doctors' time?) So they will need to pay for their own donor sperm and fertility treatment(s) which, depending on which methods they use (IUI, IVF, egg donors, extra sperm for siblings later on – there is lots to consider and pay for) and how many goes they need, and how long the whole process takes, can end up costing between £2,000 and £25,000. That's before they've even chosen the buggy.

Solo mothers will then need to support their child independently for the rest of their lives. And because they tend to be more affluent

– well educated and in well-paying jobs – in the first place, will rarely qualify for tax credits, benefits or any other kind of help from the state. But make no mistake that life for these women is brutally expensive, with all of the usual costs falling solely to them, and childcare being something they must find all of the funding for until their child, or children, reach the age when there is at least some free pre-school care. The pros of a good job and a big salary are very quickly outweighed by the cons, and the costs.

Lara is a senior manager in a government press office who has raised her twin sons alone:

> The boys are at school now and since the pandemic I've been able to work more from home. But for the first five years of their life, I had to spend every penny I earned on childcare, not only when I was at work, but if I wanted to get a haircut or go for a run or do anything for myself, I had to pay someone to look after the boys. I don't have any family except my sister who lives at the other end of the country and has her own family to look after. And because they're twins the costs are double. The nursery bills alone were £1,700 a month at one point. I worked out I was losing about £800 a month, just to keep my job.
>
> Because of my salary I didn't qualify for any help or benefits at all. I called up a helpline once to see what help I could get and when I told her what I earned the woman on the other end just laughed. I know that compared to someone on the breadline we are lucky, but at the same time it does feel like I'm stuck in a bit of a trap: earning money to spend it all on someone else looking after my children.
>
> At first I was really upset about it, but I've just had to let it go.

Another solo mum by choice, Rachel, says she feels she's not allowed to complain about the unfairness of the situation.

It cost me almost £20,000 to have Clementine. It was my life's savings. I have no help from the state and have to find the money for Clem's childcare as well as our house, car, food, everything. I earn a good salary, but I am left with nothing every month. But I feel I can't go around moaning about that because I know how hard other single mums have it.

And for Annie, as an adoptive single mother, the lack of financial support from the state is galling.

It pisses me off that if I was fostering Ebony, I would be paid quite a good salary to do so, but when you adopt you are on your own and that is obviously harder for me as a single woman than it would be if I was with someone and we were both sharing the cost of raising her. There are grants for therapy and things like that if you need them, but otherwise it's all down to me.

Don't have kids if you can't afford them, then. It's hard to escape this line. Search online for single mothers and benefits and the internet spews up pages of stories about single mothers enjoying the 'benefits lifestyle' and women who 'rake in' thousands a year on benefits but still smoke 20 a day and spend fortunes on presents at Christmas, the dreadful, generous witches. Single mothers claiming money from the state are still uniformly viewed with suspicion and mistrust, framed as thieves and layabouts. 'Unemployed single mum insists she's not a benefits sponge' said one national newspaper in December 2019.[16]

---

16 'I'm no benefits sponger': Unemployed mother with six children by three
   different fathers hits back at critics after receiving backlash from her
   stint on a reality show. www.dailymail.co.uk/femail/article-6800373/
   Single-mum-Natalee-Carucci-insists-shes-not-benefits-sponge.html

It's all a bit eugenics, isn't it, when we start telling women they can't have children because they can't afford it, or indeed for any reason? Who gets to decide who can have children and who can't? Imagine the uproar if instead we capped the number of times a year a man could have sex with a fertile woman and taxed him for it. Or banned men from selling their sperm to fertility clinics. It simply wouldn't do. Besides, despite what the press would have you believe about the lavish benefits lifestyle enjoyed by sponging single mothers, the system is actually doing a very good job of making sure they can't afford it anyway.

The British benefits system is, naturally, a big old mess and currently an even bigger shit-show than usual as it moves to replace income support, job seekers' allowance, housing benefit, child tax credit, working tax credit and every other benefit payment you've heard of with one single monthly benefit payment: Universal Credit. Universal Credit has a base allowance and then you claim other 'elements' for things like childcare and help with housing costs. It's attracted plenty of controversy due to its Stasi-like rulebook and the fact that childcare claims must be paid upfront by the parent and are reimbursed by the state, and other unrealistic expectations of people living on planet earth.

Whatever your views on Universal Credit, one thing is clear: it is disproportionately single mothers who need the help, and who suffer most, in the benefits system, whether they are in work or not, and especially in the recovery period following the coronavirus pandemic.

According to the 2020/2021 annual report on poverty by the Joseph Rowntree Foundation, over 3.5 million children in the UK live in households receiving Universal Credit. Ninety per cent of the single parents claiming Universal Credit are women. Forty-five per cent of them have jobs, but still need to claim benefits because they are trapped in low-paid, part-time or zero-hours contracts.

Even those in full-time work have seen poverty rates rise from 13 per cent in 1997 to 22 per cent in 2019.[17]

The report says: 'Lone parents continue to have the highest in-work poverty level of all family types. Single parents are disproportionately affected by barriers that prevent them escaping in-work poverty. They are more likely to be women, working in a low-wage sector, working fewer hours, and restricted by childcare and transport.'

What does in-work poverty actually mean? That someone (a single mother, in 90 per cent of Universal Credit claims) can be earning a wage and even working full time, and her income can still fall below the amount of the average weekly income. When this happens, children in these households will likely need to access food banks more regularly and miss out on the 'normal' things so many of us take for granted, like being able to do their homework on a computer at home, or being able to have the heating on in the cold. These are the families Marcus Rashford campaigned for, so that children who weren't getting a decent meal at school every day could at least continue to receive one at home during the pandemic. Not such an attractive 'benefits lifestyle' when you really look at it.

But it's not only Universal Credit and so-called handouts to people on the breadline that affect single mothers more than others. Even Child Benefit, which is, inexplicably, paid to everyone regardless of income, is set up in a way that disproportionately penalises single mothers who dare to earn good salaries. If as a parent (father or mother) you earn over £50k you are actively encouraged by HMRC to opt not to receive Child Benefit (although it is not enforced). So, if you are a single mother earning over £50k and because you have a conscience you opt out, you do not receive Child Benefit. But if you are a couple and you each earn over £50k, your household

17 Joseph Rowntree Foundation (2021) *UK Poverty 2020/21: The Leading Independent Report.* York: Joseph Rowntree Foundation.

income can be £100k before you need to consider opting out of receiving Child Benefit. Put simply, if you are a couple and well-off, the greater your scope for receiving Child Benefit. If you are a single mother who dares to earn the big bucks and live alone, you are expected to say goodbye to it a lot sooner.

The state also gives tax breaks to married people. The marriage tax allowance lets couples transfer an amount of their tax allowance to their spouse, giving couples a discount on their tax, relative to single people. Whether or not you find it really quite sinister that the state effectively rewards women who get married, the marriage tax allowance affects single mothers disproportionately, as they are more likely to stay single while men remarry and give their new wife the tax break.

Even the fun stuff is made harder for single parents. Hotels and holiday operators still base most of their room costs on double occupancy, so that as with the council tax, the single person in fact pays a premium for being unmarried. Factor in travel, meals, treats… it's no coincidence that the children and I have mostly been camping since their dad and I split up. And at most major tourist attractions, from Harry Potter World to Flamingoland, you'll find family tickets for two adults and a sorry single parent 'discount' option that seems to laugh at you judgingly as you push through the turnstiles. (Shout-out to the National Trust, which offers family tickets for families with one adult for exactly half of the cost for two. If they can do it, why don't other places?)

The system still runs on a married-is-best model, and if you are feeling particularly fed up with this fact, you can begin to legitimately argue that literally EVERYTHING IN THE WORLD is charged at a premium rate for single parents, who don't have the benefit of another household income, and especially single mothers, who tend typically to have lower incomes because of their child-raising commitments.

The coronavirus pandemic of 2019 was not kind to single parents either, and many who were already struggling financially found themselves facing even bigger, darker challenges. *Tackling single parent poverty after coronavirus*, an interim report from the Learning and Work Institute, Gingerbread and the Joseph Rowntree Foundation, published in December 2020, found that single parents were more likely to have lost their jobs during the pandemic, with one in ten becoming unemployed. They were also more likely to have been furloughed: one in three (34 per cent) single parents were furloughed, compared to just one in four (25 per cent) coupled parents.[18]

Among other depressing statistics, the report found that single parent families were also over three times as likely to have used food banks, with single parents more likely than other parents to be stuck in part-time, low-paid work. This meant that nearly half (44 per cent) of children in a single parent family were living in poverty during the crisis, compared to just one in four (26 per cent) of those living in couple-parented families.

Is it any wonder single mothers need benefits? Moreover, do we really begrudge them the help? Even if they aren't working, perhaps because their baby is too young or their children are at different ages, is their motherhood not in fact a kind of work, which allows the other parent to work? Whether or not they live in the same house shouldn't really make any difference. Without the work of motherhood, half of the nation (the fathers) wouldn't be able to go to work at all. Founder of the Women's Equality Party, Sandi Toksvig, calls this our country's GUDP (Grossly Undervalued Domestic Product): the caring, support and childcare women do, without seeing a penny.

---

18 Joe Dromey, Laura Dewar and Jerome Finnegan (2020) *Tackling single parent poverty after coronavirus*. Leicester: Learning and Work Institute.

But what about child maintenance? Surely that helps? Well, yes, but again mostly no. Firstly, no, not at all if you are a solo mother by choice and no other parent is responsible for your child. If you are a parent who is separated or divorced, or you know who the father of your child is, the law in the UK states that you are both financially responsible for your child or children. So the parent who moves out, or who has them less than the other parent, should still make a contribution to their own children's running costs.

But unless you have managed to time your separation to occur at exactly the same moment that your ex gets a massive pay rise, or wins the rollover week on the EuroMillions, they won't necessarily have all that much to spare. Because they will also need to live somewhere else and begin to incur all of their own bills and running costs in their new home. As my solicitor advised me wearily, having clearly seen the incredulous look on my face a few times before: they can't give you money they haven't got.

And as if it isn't exasperating enough when the numbers begin to leak from every orifice, the Child Maintenance Service (formerly the Child Support Agency) has developed a really unhelpful online calculator that 'helps' you work out what that child maintenance amount should be. This calculator 'gives you an amount to discuss with the other parent if you are arranging child maintenance yourselves'.[19]

I can't imagine there have been many successful discussions between separating parents using this calculator. Bearing in mind that it is almost impossible to divide up the life of a child and the blessed domestic load by nights of the week, since it mostly lives in a woman's head, and the fact that the paying parent may not be feeling inclined to be all that generous with their wages to you, the human manifestation of all their woes, how can an online calculator

---

19 Calculate your child maintenance. www.gov.uk/calculate-child-maintenance

with all the technological sophistication of a Fisher-Price shop till make any helpful suggestions? It also seems to have been developed by someone who last went to Tesco in 1809 and imagines children need only eat gruel and play with sticks.

Of all the single mothers I have spoken to, precisely none find it helpful or fair, as it typically suggests a very low and unrealistic amount of child maintenance that is more concerned with the payers' income than the cost of raising the children, and vitriolic exes can wave it around in their defence when they're not feeling inclined to splash their cash (which, if you happen to be feeling feministy again, it is worth remembering they can often only earn because someone else – that's you, muggins – is looking after their children).

The fact that it is a suggestion, and not an official figure ordained by the state, seems to get lost somewhere in translation, and I have heard countless stories of men (sorry, but it is always the men; that's not misandry it's just the facts – I've never met a man yet who complains his child maintenance payments are simply too low) who earn far more than their exes and look after their children far less, paying the bare minimum suggested by the calculator, simply because they don't want to play nicely and IT SAYS ON THE CALCULATOR.

Catherine works part-time as a communications manager and lives in a three-bedroom house with her two teenage sons. Her ex and the father of her sons is a retail manager. He works full time and lives in a two-bedroom flat where he has the boys, in theory, for two nights a week. Despite the fact he earns significantly more than Catherine and has his children significantly less, he pays the bare minimum maintenance suggested by the calculator – £200 a month per child:

> It just doesn't touch the sides. Once you've paid for bus fare and school lunches there's very little left. They hardly even

went there at all during the pandemic, and my eldest still won't go there, but he made no adjustments for this. His argument was that it was his choice; he was providing accommodation.

It feels so unfair. It shouldn't be something he can hide behind. The way it works it out on nights per week and salaries just doesn't seem to bear any relation to the everyday costs of rearing a child, or our particular circumstances. It seems to be all about him and not the children.

I don't argue it though, because I know there's no point. It's all based on goodwill at the end of the day, and we don't have a lot of that.

And if you are unlucky enough to find yourself at the mercy of an ex who doesn't want to pay maintenance for their child, the CMS offers a Pay and Collect service. This sounds helpful and reasonable: the government will step in like a superhero and make sure your child gets the parental funding that is their right under British law. Only here's the rub: the state takes 4 per cent of your child's maintenance for the service of collecting the maintenance. Your child pays the state a collection fee in order to receive the maintenance that buys their food and keeps them warm. The Bastard Act of 1576 still echoes down the years.

So the unfortunate truth is that unless you actually really *are* Heather Mills-McCartney or the former Mrs Bezos, or have somehow managed to build your Bitcoin empire while you were birthing and breastfeeding the children, there are probably going to be some very significant shortfalls in the equation on every side.

Things just do not add up.

In *The Road Less Travelled*, the world's bestselling self-help book, M. Scott Peck opens with this line (which in a post-Trump era reads kind of funny but wasn't meant to be when Peck wrote it in 1978): 'Life is difficult. This is a great truth, one of the greatest truths. It is a great truth because once we truly see this truth, we transcend it.'[20]

This is not to suggest that all you need to do is transcend your financial worries and life will be great. But accepting early on that nothing about being a single parent, especially a mother in a patriarchy that still runs on a male-breadwinner model, is financially rewarding might help you deal with some of the surprising realities that you are going to encounter. Life and what you can do in it is going to change. Your card may get declined in the supermarket. Learn to live with this early on and you may find the whole thing less stressful than I did.

Because for a long time, I fought it. Despite all the evidence mounting around me, I refused to accept that my romantic attachment, or lack of, was somehow now dictating my financial status. I was without a husband; I had missed my target and had lost my bonus as a result. I raged at the humiliation of it. I raged that on more than one occasion I had to ask for help. I am forever grateful that I could.

I had kindly sisters, my mum and friends who could help. Sometimes in the very early days, when I was still working out how on earth we'd survive, I'd leave my mum's house with a carrier bag full of food as though I had just been to Morrison's. We laughed about it, but inside I was pure shame. I was failing to thrive. Now I understood why we had a charity and why so many single mothers needed benefits. It is very difficult to make things add up alone.

And I had it easy. I not only had support but children who were old enough to be at school for large parts of the year. I had work and an income. I had the house, and their dad who paid his maintenance and was always nearby to help with perilous trips to the

---

20 M. Scott Peck (1990) *The Road Less Travelled: A New Psychology of Love, Traditional Values and Spiritual Growth* (originally published 1978). London: Arrow Books, page 3.

supermarket. Some single mothers don't have the luxury of family nearby or exes who want to share the financial burden.

'When I got pregnant, he made it very clear he wasn't going to be a part of Alfie's life,' says Jo.

> As far as he was concerned it was a mistake, he didn't ask for it and he wanted nothing to do with it. He has never paid a penny towards his son. I haven't even tried going down the CMS route because he's now a full-time student, so I know he won't have to pay anything. I have given up on sharing the costs. The only good thing is I have total control over what happens in our lives. I don't have to consult him on anything. This is my family: me and Alfie.

I felt I might rage forever. At one point I considered becoming an MP, another time I was going to be a human rights divorce lawyer. Watching my married/cohabiting, dual-income friends buy bigger and better houses and go on longer-haul holidays didn't help either. My contemporaries were buying huge, high-ceilinged 'projects' with summer houses and basements and giant glass-box extensions. Perhaps I have too many wealthy friends. But even the less wealthy married friends seem to push ahead somehow: outdoor kitchens and loft conversions, gyms and driveways. Two incomes in one household go a lot further than one – there is no getting around it. I won't pretend I don't covet these homes and all their improvements at times. Of course I want these places; of course I have to swallow a bitter little pill every time I find myself there, of course.

But a part of me wonders if perhaps I've just never really wanted to be that kind of well-off. Not if it means paying with my authentic self. And I wonder if perhaps this is a common feeling among single mothers who actively choose to do it by themselves, a decision not to check into the five-star hotel, but to seek out the funny little guesthouse down the road.

The financials of single motherhood are complex and exhausting. We are at the centre of a big ugly Venn diagram involving economics, gender politics, time, culture, mother nature and a bunch of other dodgy characters no one invited to the party. But! All is not lost. Despite everything I've just told you, there are some good – dare I say priceless – aspects of the financial situation we single mothers can find ourselves in.

Single-mumpreneurs

For one thing, we make great entrepreneurs.

The financial outlook for single mothers can sound so miserable that it is almost tempting to get married again. And plenty of us do. But lots of single and solo mums find the skills they acquire and develop on the parenting frontline can also drive them to find success in business and their careers.

Like all good news, positive stories about single mothers building amazing businesses, creating incredible art and making loads of money don't often make the headlines (although Hollywood does love a single-mother-against-the-world story in the vein of *Mildred Pierce* and more recently, *Maid*). But there are plenty of women who have turned their single mother rags to great riches in real life.

We all know by now how the author J.K. Rowling famously wrote her Harry Potter books while she was a single mother living on benefits, writing her books in the cafes of Edinburgh while her baby slept in her pram by her side. Other famous single mums of note include, in the US, the voice-actor Pamela Adlon, who based her now multi-award-winning show *Better Things* on her life as a single mum raising three daughters. Sheryl Sandberg, founder of Huffington Post and now the COO at Facebook, wrote her book *Option B* after her husband died unexpectedly and she found herself a single mum.[21] Erin Brockovich's story, the single mother and legal clerk who successfully brought a case against Pacific Gas and Electric in California for contamination of water, was made into a film starring Julia Roberts. Time100's 2021 list of the world's most influential people included another campaigning single mum, Phyllis Omido from Mombasa, who led her community's fight to close the lead-smelting plant where she worked after she realised her own breast milk was poisoning her son.

There is something in the lack of other options – the need to succeed no matter what, the no going back – that drives single mothers to create and achieve.

Julie Hawkins founded the Single Mums Business Network (SMBN) as a way of meeting other single mums in the same situation as her. She describes how, when her marriage ended, she lost her job because she couldn't work the hours that her employer wanted her to.

> I had to choose between my child and my career; I chose my child and lost my home. Overnight, I went from being a married, 20-year-career-girl who owned her own home to a single mum with a repossessed property and a damaged credit score, turned away by landlords and lenders due to my status.
>
> It was humiliating and degrading. I did have to claim benefits for a while; there was no other way I could make ends meet. And it is really hard to find work that pays enough and syncs with your childcare and school holidays. But my work ethic has always been really strong. I set up my own business, selling a pregnancy cushion I designed that supports women in different stages of pregnancy, and I did a law degree to improve my prospects and just kept fighting. I eventually got to the stage where I did a trade show at

21 Sheryl Sandberg and Adam Grant (2019) *Option B: Facing Adversity, Building Resilience, and Finding Joy.* London: Penguin.

the NEC with the cushion and it boosted my sales, and I was able to come off the benefits. And weirdly I found that being single gave me more time, especially in the evenings, to really push myself.

So many of SMBN's members are really strong, independent women who absolutely have not chosen a 'benefits lifestyle'. Some of them do have benefits to top up their income, but there's often no other way around it when you are running a household with children on one income. It's not something they pick for a career. They are just not the stereotype that gets put out there in the media. They just want to work and hold their heads up high, look nice, feel nice. Some of them are at the top of their game, turning six figures, others are just starting out on their journey. What they all share is that grit and determination not to become what everyone else seems to expect of them.

She set up the network, she says, because she wanted to meet other single mums who wanted to work hard and who needed the PR and support that a business network provides.

As a group we've got so much to say. Now we've got over 50 members and we have events and awards and publish a magazine. Everyone pays a fee to be a member – it's not a charity and it's not subsidised; that has always been really important to me.

Having a high tolerance for ambiguity – not knowing where the next cheque is coming from and being able to deal with whatever comes your way – turns out to be a quality that makes single mums good entrepreneurs. A 2016 study from the University of Malaysia looked at the link between motivation and passion, and the entrepreneurial success of single mothers. It said:

Entrepreneurs continually face more uncertainty in their every-day environment than do managers of established organizations;

entrepreneurs who remain in their jobs are likely to score high on tests for this trait... the entrepreneurs who have a low tolerance for ambiguity, will experience stress, react prematurely, avoid ambiguity and seek certainty... as entrepreneurs they [single mothers]... will experience ambiguous situations as challenging, desirable and interesting. These situations require individuals to think creatively and construct an innovative approach due to changes and problems...[22]

And of course single mums are grafters. Aruna Bansal set up the Asian Single Parents' Network when she found herself looking for friends in similar circumstances. She says:

Single mums have an incredible work ethic, juggling a number of tasks simultaneously as they don't have a partner to fall back on. They have no choice but to get on with things and do their best to make things work. It also makes you determined, resilient and fearless when you have difficult decisions to make. All great qualities when running a business.

I like the idea of single mothers being entrepreneurs, women who walk a different path and create new byways in the process. In business, people talk so positively about mavericks and original thinkers and those who think outside the box; we give them grants and mentors and celebrate their successes at awards ceremonies and on reality shows. We buy their inspirational and motivational books and listen to their podcasts. Yet when it comes to single mothers, so many of whom live their entire lives outside the box and think original thoughts for breakfast, lunch and dinner, our culture still

22 Paraphrased from Irwan Ismail et al. (2016) Entrepreneurial success among single mothers: the role of motivation and passion. *Procedia Economics and Finance 37*, page 123.

frames them as the undesirable option at best; at worst, spongers and layabouts.

When we know that so much of a child's early developmental experience is defined by their financial situation, I find it unfathomable that we are still making life so hard for the women who raise our children, simply because they're not attached to a man. I wonder how things would change if, instead of slowly starving single mothers and their children, we backed them with kindness and support and the kind of financial faith we give to businesses and start-ups across the land.

Martha's daughter was a baby when her father left and moved to a city over two hours away from where Martha lives.

> He wanted to have the baby every few days so I was driving back and forth with her and having to hand her over at the motorway services even while I was still breastfeeding – it was really traumatic.
>
> I'd been a chef with a fairly steady income and regular hours before I'd had her but there was no way I could work the same kind of hours afterwards, especially with all the driving and the on-off schedule we had. I didn't really have a choice but to be self-employed; I didn't want to live on income support and getting a 'normal' job would just not have been possible with childcare.
>
> So I started sewing. At first I did cushions and made a few bits and pieces for children; people started asking me to make things for them and I found I was making all sorts of things like aprons and washbags. I'd also started buying second-hand cashmere jumpers in the charity shops to make trousers for babies, and one day had the idea to make recycled cashmere wrist-warmers because they were smaller and used less material. I designed my own pattern that can make a pair of warmers out of a jumper and started selling them online in my Etsy

shop. On the weekends my daughter was with her dad, I sold them at my local market. Things just kind of grew from there. I realised I needed to really focus on the wrist-warmers so I stopped making other things and honed in on what I was doing. I started dying and upcycling my own cashmere so I could have my own colours rather than just what I found in the charity shops. I got some nice labels made and made it look and feel like a real brand. And I started promoting the warmers on Instagram and social media. I think being able to promote myself and my product on social media really helped; I didn't have to spend a lot of money on advertising or marketing. It's amazing really. Horrendous but also amazing.

I've just moved the whole operation into a new studio and I'm at the point where I am thinking about taking someone on to help. I sell my wrist-warmers in five stores and in my Etsy store, and I'm really feeling like there are not enough hours in the day. My daughter is still at primary school, and I have to pick her up so I usually only get six hours in my studio and I'm working all hours at home as well. This morning I was dying cashmere at seven o'clock before school, and then when we got home I was photographing new wrist-warmers for the site.

There is no off-switch and sometimes I get home and think how lovely it would be if someone had made me dinner for once. But I am independent and don't have to answer to anyone, and I'm really proud of myself for having this proper business and actually earning decent money from it. I've always thought being an entrepreneur was for other people. I didn't sit there as a girl and think: *I want to be a single mum with my own wrist-warmer business when I grow up.* It's grown out of necessity and because it could work with my responsibilities as a mum. But I'm just starting to feel like I can celebrate all I've achieved. I've built a real business based on making something out of nothing; it feels like a nice little magic trick.

A life more streamlined

But even if you don't have a business to launch or an Instagram following to cultivate, if you have not a single entrepreneurial bone in your body, the single mum lifestyle doesn't always need to seem so bleak.

Susan Golombok said that when the gold-standard is the male-led nuclear family, the research tends to focus on the absence of negatives rather than the presence of positives. What if we think so hard about what we haven't got or can't have that we don't see the things we are already rich in? What positives can single mothers, who are busy choking on all those bitter pills and great difficult truths, find in their situation?

There will be no evangelising here about the rewards of self-sufficiency or off-grid living. We had chickens for a while and having all those extra eggs around the place drove me nuts; I came to balk at even just the thought of an omelette. No, this is not about having clothes swaps or foraging for berries, or sharing the cost of rearing and butchering a pig with a few other local families, although of course all of those things are nice and good if you have the time.

But there is plenty to be enjoyed in a streamlined life, without the trappings of affluence and all its complexities and waste.

With a smaller bank balance and the same small house we have always lived in (you will not meet many single mothers while crawling up the property ladder) I have less space to clean and fewer people to pay, no cleaning service or gardener or Farrow & Ball colour consultancy. I have smaller food bills. I have no tailored pet-food subscriptions, no gym memberships, no car finance, no private healthcare or dental fees, no credit card reward schemes, no pay-monthly beauty-buying clubs, no wine clubs, no golf clubs, no club clubs and no on-demand home fitness training systems in my list of Bluetooth devices. No deathly evenings spent discussing the virtues of stocks and shares ISAs over cash with financial advisors. I rarely fly anywhere, it being expensive to travel, and my car is my mum's old Polo with a 1.4 engine that my daughter says smells like a disease. (A useful by-product of being poor is that your carbon footprint remains piously low, without even trying.) Everything is reduced. My life is small – it's miniscule! But that's not always a bad thing. In fact it's kind of aspirational, when you really think about it.

Kate Humble writes in her book *A Year of Living Simply*: 'Contentment and simplicity are intrinsic. The reason so many of us in Western society are not content, is that we live lives that are overcrowded and over complicated. We've confused simplicity with convenience. But convenience doesn't seem to bring happiness.'[23]

Kate speaks the humble truth. Across the world, movements like tiny living and minimalism, espoused by the likes of Marie Kondo and Shira Gill, have gained popularity over the last decade as human beings realise what a mess we've made of things and try desperately to find new, less selfish ways to live on the planet before it bursts. And if what we stressed-out Westerners – with our forest-bathing and sound-baths, our journaling and our weekend yoga retreats – are all really craving is a return to a more simple, downsized, uncluttered life, then I think me and all the single mums might already be living it. It may not be the kind of textbook tiny or sleek, shiny minimal they make TV lifestyle shows about, but it is by its nature a more simple way of life.

I wouldn't ever dream of suggesting I'm deliriously content (anyone who knows me would immediately tell you otherwise) or pretend that the financial hardship endured by so many single parent families is an aspirational lifestyle (although there are plenty of us doing style on a budget, and some of us, like tin-can chef and single mum Jack Monroe, are making a name for ourselves in the

23 Kate Humble (2020) *A Year of Living Simply: The Joys of a Life Less Complicated*. London: Aster, page 41.

process). But I do know that I can happily live *without* the extra discontent that a life more complicated can bring.

And while I do not in any way claim to do it well, or suggest that the finances are not a source of constant worry to me (I have had to ask for help on many occasions and made some fantastically stupid decisions along the way, still do), I am increasingly rewarded by the simple thought that it is a problem all of my own, that I am responsible for and that only I can fix. That is the real payback.

Money is something we still talk so little about, especially as women. When we have it we pretend we haven't got any, and when we don't have it we pretend we do. We have nothing in our accounts, but we max out at Klarna and offer to buy everyone lunch all the same. We seem to have such a lot of shame around money. Perhaps another hangover from the days when we needed to be looked after by a man. And perhaps why no one ever tells you how good it feels to be in charge of it and not have it be in charge of you. The sense of achievement that comes when you clear a debt or pay off a bill, book your own holiday or give your children their pocket money. No one talks about the joy or the empowerment that comes from saying no to something because that's the right thing to do, or yes to something because you can, from paying into your own pension to holding your own purse strings all by yourself, even when they are only very short.

It's difficult and confusing and often overwhelming at times to have all of the financial responsibility. And yet somehow that feels better to me than my finances being mixed up with love and sex and power and someone else: with being married. In this sense, becoming a single mother and having to manage my own finances, and that of my children, has been a journey of self-discovery every bit as revealing, gut-wrenching and ultimately emancipating as any counselling or therapy.

I have had to face some fairly hefty demons, examine my own behaviours around money and, in some cases, try to change some very deeply ingrained spending habits. I have had to become the person who splits the hairs a little bit when the restaurant bill comes at the end of the night. I've had to learn to delay gratification (work in progress) and to educate myself about all sorts of boring things like switching suppliers, combining pension pots, why it makes no sense to save while you've still got debts, how to remortgage, how to negotiate, how to ask for discounts. I've decluttered and capsule-wardrobed and eBayed the absolute living shit out of everything I own, or owned.

But when life is complicated in other areas, having a simplified, less complicated financial situation on your hands – especially if it's yours and yours only – can be a strange source of comfort. An element of control in an otherwise unpredictable existence.

It's also worth remembering that affluence has its downsides too. We just don't like to talk about it so much, because then what would we do? What would we all be striving for if not affluence?

There is zero comfort to be found in the misery of others, but remembering that affluence and all its trappings don't automatically guarantee happiness or better outcomes for anyone can at least bring some balance to the conversation for single mothers facing financial downturn and worrying about the impact on their children's future.

In his book *Affluenza*, the psychologist Oliver James examines the rising levels of emotional distress in children and young people in wealthy Western societies. He describes a study into the emotional wellbeing of teenagers, from 2003:

> The study looked at levels of anxiety and depression in two very large (5000 plus) representative samples of fifteen year olds, one in 1987 and the other in 1999. Amongst the bottom social class, girls' rates rose only a little but in the top class, the rise was from 24 per cent in 1987 to 38 per cent in 1999 – more than one-third of the most privileged.

> Excellent academic performance of high-income girls cor-
> related with ill-being.[24]

It's not an especially rewarding exercise, searching for proof that being better off makes your children ill-er in the head. But it can be helpful to remember sometimes when you are feeling frustrated by your lack of perceived 'progress' in life as a single-income parent. The grass really isn't greener on the other side; it's just a different length and sometimes even harder to mow.

The lockdowns of 2020 brought this home for me. With life stripped back to its bare essentials, there was no need or opportunity for days out, no occasion to notice other people's abundance or compare ourselves to wealthier families much at all. Everyone was in the same prison, and we all had the same release: a bike ride, a walk in the park or by the sea, a Zoom call with friends. And on those Zooms, we were all just heads on a screen. It was in many ways a great leveller; we were all the same. And when it came to the things we really needed to survive – a home, our friends, open space on our doorstep to explore and each other – we were already extremely rich indeed.

A few thoughts on saving the pennies, from one single mum to another

- If you've got debts, no matter how large or small, it is always best to try to pay them off before you start trying to save. Banks charge you more interest on debt than they give you on capital, so this is a no-brainer. It may not be as exciting to clear a debt as it is to spend or save, but being debt free is

24 Oliver James (2007) *Affluenza: How to Be Successful* and *Stay Sane*. London: Vermilion.

pretty sweet! Try giving yourself a little (inexpensive) reward every time you pay off some debt to motivate yourself, and keep going until it's all gone. (And if debt is starting to become a problem and you are feeling overwhelmed, the debt charity StepChange can really help you get back on track.)

- De-clutter and sell what you don't need. Even if it's only a few pounds for an old scooter it is better in your bank account than cluttering up the porch. Facebook Marketplace, eBay, Gumtree and Vinterior are your friends. People even come and collect things! Try to make it a regular habit so that you get used to doing it and that little bit extra is coming in all the time. Local neighbourhood WhatsApp groups and apps like Nextdoor are also a great way to borrow and share things with people close by.

- Get smart about the food shop. Plan your meals and then write a shopping list and stick to it. Top tip: the 'deals' that hit you in the face when you walk into the shop are not always the best prices. Head into the aisles and see what else is available before you put anything in your basket. And buying veg loose is always cheaper than the pre-packed stuff. And of course going shopping when you are hungry is a major no-no.

- Ask for discounts. This is major! Don't ask really does mean you don't get. Whether you are getting a quote for insurance or booking a holiday, it is always worth getting on the phone and talking to a human being and explaining you are on a single income and asking if they can better their price. Very often you'll find they will, and the person on the end of the phone will be delighted they could help.

- It's hard to get out to an exercise class in the evening when you have small children, plus gym memberships are expensive. Kill two birds with one stone by committing to walk more, whether it's to school or work or both. You save money on the gym and petrol, and it's better for the environment. There are also loads of free online exercise classes. I really like Lucy Wyndham Read's 7-minute workouts. Even I can't find an excuse to miss a 7-minute exercise class.

- Talk to your local Citizens Advice Bureau and/or Ginger-bread about what discounts and benefits are available to you. You might find you are eligible for something you have never heard of, for example if you are also caring for an elderly relative or you are a widow, so it's definitely worth doing this. And if you feel funny about accepting help, try to see it as an investment in yourself and your future. You are definitely not scrounging!

- Use a spending tracker. I know, I know, really boring. But it takes five minutes to set up and once it's up and running you'll find you use it all the time. It doesn't have to be in Excel or fancy software; just draw a table with what's coming in and what's going out and then do the maths. Even if you don't stick rigidly to it, it's a helpful way of staying aware of what you're spending and getting to know your own habits.

- Get a pension! Women, especially those of us born to Generation X (born between 1965 and 1980) are facing major shortfalls in our projected retirement income. It is better to start early but that said it is also never too late to start, and there are loads of apps now that make the whole pensions thing much easier to manage, especially if you have odd bits or pensions here and there from different jobs. Pensions are financial self-care: looking after your future self just in case you don't become a millionaire in the meantime.

CHAPTER FOUR

Who Will Want You?

The definition of insanity is doing the same thing over
and over and expecting different results.
Unknown

The only regret I've had in my life is not shagging
the men who wanted to shag me.
Kathy Burke, *All Woman*

My mum had been thinking in old money when she asked that most
rhetorical of questions: 'Who will want you, with two children?'

She had momentarily forgotten half a century of feminist progress
that meant women don't need keeping by men any more, and that
even as a wretched wastrel with two offspring by another sire, I
might still be able to pull.

I knew plenty of people, myself for example, who were the
children of perfectly happy second marriages and blended families.
This was hardly a new thing. So I wasn't worried about being able to
meet someone or have a new relationship now that I was a scandalous
divorcee. Or rather, that wasn't the thing that worried me most.

She also hadn't factored in the 24-hour disco-sex-party-for-hot-
single-mums-in-your-area that is online dating. It wasn't around
in her day. It had hardly been around in mine, not before I got
married anyway. We had met the old-fashioned way, in a pub. He

was younger than me, so we had both watched curiously at first, then with increasing envy, as his friends began to meet their new partners online. Although it would still be a number of years before Tinder, it still seemed incredible to imagine that people would post pictures of themselves on websites, on the internet for everyone to see, and admit that they were sad and single. Good God.

Still, by the time I was ready to think about meeting someone new, online dating was normal. Everyone was at it. I signed up to the matchmaking service of a well-known national newspaper, wrote some lies about having hobbies and how I loved exercise, and watched agog as the messages poured in from unsuitable men all around the country.

The first person I chatted to and met up with was a psycho-therapist who lived in Scotland. He had the look of someone who had partied too hard in the 90s – various teeth were missing – and he told me early on in our discussions that he had regular enemas. And although he said he was a psychotherapist, he rarely seemed to have any clients or do any work at all. Still, I didn't let any of that bother me and fell immediately in love with this out-and-out catch who lived about eight hours away and didn't seem particularly bothered about me. The idea of having my own personal counsellor seemed attractive and what was a little distance between two people who were so very clearly meant to be together? It didn't last. I look back at myself and wonder what on earth I was thinking. The only explanation I can find is that I was at that time a kind of lunatic who had recently escaped from the asylum.

The next attempt was someone in entertainment whose children were a similar age to mine and, although he lived too far away, seemed like he could be a good match. He was outrageous and funny and pursued me in a way I'd never really experienced – buying tickets to shows without even asking if I wanted to go and whisking me off to parties with celebrities and free champagne. A wizard with words, he sent intoxicating messages about needing me so much that he wanted to be inside my cell structure. No one had said things like that to me before and I drank it all up. But I threw it back up again when he revealed himself to be a sociopath who wanted to control what I wore and what I ate, and, among many other horrible behaviours, regularly defamed his poor ex-wife on social media.

There have been a few relationships in the eight years since then. My best friend says no one can accuse me of having a type. There was a former flame (everyone needs to revisit an ex, it's what Facebook was invented for). A scientist, who explained pensions to me and always had reusable bags in the car for when he went to the supermarket. A lecturer who fancied himself far more than I did.

Nothing has, as yet, worked out. If by working out what we mean is: lasting a long time or showing any signs of becoming the fabled second-time around (how on earth Elizabeth Taylor managed six I really don't know). But, long or short, they have all been important and meaningful experiences that, even if they stung at times, I'm glad have happened.

Meeting people really isn't the problem – although I do get nostalgic for when you saw people you fancied in the pub instead of in your phone, and as far as fun-things-to-do go, writing dating profiles is on a par for me with emptying the food waste bin – it is making things stick that is the tricky part.

Romance before you had children was only about the two of you, but now you have a whole set of mis-matching children and a bunch of vitriolic exes, and probably quite a few dogs to factor in. Just the logistics are mind-bending. You both have jobs and busy lives and schedules with your exes that do not correlate. Your evenings are punctuated by pick-ups and drop-offs to various children's clubs and activities, so that syncing your lives becomes another game of Tetris and you find you can only spend time together every third Tuesday between six and seven o'clock in the evening, and then only in term-time, in a car park.

And you have to get used to a new person and all of their habits, something that gets harder as you get older and more curmudgeonly anyway and is doubly hard when you're just not used to the physical presence of another body around the place. One friend told of a lovely guy who ticked loads of her boxes but who did a really loud and rather upsetting poo every morning. It was in the en suite off her bedroom, so there was no escaping it. After flushing he would come back to bed and never acknowledge that it had happened. Facing a future where that was her morning alarm for the next 40 years, she decided to get out before it was too late.

And then there are the children. I admit I found involving the children to be a less complicated affair when they were small. Young children will think a man is a keeper if he turns up with Bean Boozled and a packet of crisps. They are less easy to please as they get older. Teenagers, in particular, can be exceptionally critical of your choices. You might want to keep a new romance away from a teenager, but only for a quiet life, not because you are doing anything inherently wrong.

Different children bring different situations. One friend has a daughter with autism who really struggles when people she's not familiar with are in her home. So my friend goes every other weekend to her boyfriend's house. She says:

> It was great at first and I felt like I was going on holiday; I get cooked for and really enjoy the escape. But increasingly I feel bad about leaving the house; all the jobs mount up, I don't have the time to be away so often.

For children who have never experienced a man living in the house, the novelty doesn't so much wear off as never exist in the first place. When Lara's new boyfriend popped round for a cup of tea, her son said after a few minutes, loudly and in front of him: 'Can that man go now?'

Whatever the set of challenges are, a common thread seems to be a sense of feeling torn between the children and the relationship, and life, especially if the relationship lives a distance away and there is a need to leave home for periods of time. While many single mothers do get time off when their children are with the other parent, it isn't always easy to compartmentalise a new relationship into your specific windows of free time when you might have many other things that need doing. I've heard over and over single mums come to the conclusion that a serious relationship can't and won't happen until the children leave home. Not because they don't meet nice partners, or have plenty of fun in the meantime, but because they don't have the mental energy or space to fit everyone in.

Fiona, a solo mum with a teenage son, says: 'When he leaves home I can see myself going on those walking holidays for single people. I'd like that. But until then I'm not really bothered. Between work and home I don't know where I'd find the time.'

Lara says:

> For the first five years of their life, any free time I had was about me and looking after myself. I didn't have the emotional bandwidth for a relationship. I have started dating again recently and I'm enjoying it, but part of me also regrets coming out of my sexual and emotional dormancy. I was quite happy there.

So many stars need to align in order to make things work. I've learnt there is no secret to success, and no perfect conditions can be established for romance to flourish. Everyone's circumstances are different and ever-changing. External influences you didn't even think about before – a new job, an elderly parent, a gender-queer child, an unhappy ex – these things can swing in on a dirty great wrecking ball and send all your carefully constructed relationship pieces flying. The search for love when you have children and a backstory is like that wobbly floor ride at the fair: you're never sure where your feet are going to land next.

I guess it depends on the kind of person you are, and how much you like fairground rides. But if you can lose the imperative to see new relationships as potential life partners (and if you can get everyone you know to stop asking if he's a keeper) and basically do away with the second-time-around thing and see it more as a first-time-for-everything thing, then dating on this side of the marriage and children fence can be hilarious, exhilarating and completely and utterly fascinating.

People coming out of their own personal hells have a lot of baggage, it's true. And it can be a pain to lug that stuff around; I've learned the hard way not to assign myself the role of baggage handler any more. But the good thing about baggage is that it's usually full of all the best things in life that we love so much we can't leave home without them. Our best outfits and our favourite books, our comfort blankets, our sex toys.

And because of all the treasures they carry around with them, people with baggage can also be some of the most interesting people in the room. Yes, there are a number of cliches to be observed in the single parent dating pool – people inexplicably stand-up paddleboarding everywhere – but in reality what it makes for is a bunch of people who are really very good company and have loads of great chat.

They're also often imbued with a sense of devil-may-care. Having been in unhappy marriages and relationships for years, or with children who are older and less demanding than they used to be, many of the people you meet on the dating scene are like butterflies shedding their chrysalises. People who are emerging from years of repression and unmet needs, inactive sex lives, buried desires, who have come through great tragedies and weathered unholy storms, who are reclaiming their sense of self or simply opening their eyes to new ways of being.

All the stories. My friends love to hear about my misadventures in dating ('did you shag him?' and 'has he got a big cock?' generally being the first questions they tend to ask, especially the married/cohabiting ones). And I always enjoy hearing the stories of the men I meet on dates and from friends who are also dating. Some of course are sad, like the woman who had an affair with the guy's best friend so that he didn't only lose his marriage but his best mate too. And the ex who stabbed himself in the head with a fork in front of the children – how do you begin to handle that scene in the kitchen? But just as often they are hilarious. The guy whose ex-wife had bought her son a vacuum cleaner for his bedroom as a birthday present (she really tickled me). The self-styled Viking who had a miniature Valhalla fire pit in his garden. The hunk who lived in the woods and caught fish for his tea but talked like Worzel Gummidge.

As a child I watched Billy Wilder's 1967 *Some Like it Hot* on repeat. At the start of the film, we meet a group of prohibition-era gangsters who are posing as funeral directors: Rigoletto's. Sombre organ music plays as a detective enters the funeral parlour. 'I'm here for the old lady's funeral,' he says, to the uncommonly large forbearers on the door. The heavy satin curtains open, and instead of the weeping congregation we expect, we find ourselves thrust into a jumping speakeasy, all freaks and dancing girls and hot jazz.

Dating after being married feels, at times, like walking into Rigoletto's. Unregulated.

So much of this bonkers underworld might not have come my way, had I stayed married. One – reasonably normal – date asked me: 'Did you ever imagine you'd be sitting here on a first date when you were 45?' I could only answer that I was just happy to be sitting there, discovering someone new and finding out about their world, rather than watching to the end of Netflix at home with someone I have run out of things to talk about with.

Dating after kids and marriage is of course more than a series of hilarious mis-haps and stories to dine out on. Great relationships can and do happen after divorce and after children.

With all that life experience under their belts and all those hard lessons learned, many people find themselves having had an emotional upgrade. Maybe they are better at expressing their feelings or about allowing their partners to keep their own space. Maybe they are kinder or more patient, with more well-established lifestyles and expectations. Or they are just broader churches all round.

As one man I met put it:

> The separation opened up a can of worms for me. There was clearly work to do, so I set about trying to know myself better and change. Not easy, but necessary, I thought. All I know is that communication, truth and self-awareness must be the way not only to have a relationship but to live one's life. I still don't know if I'm any good in a relationship, or good enough, but I know that if I stick to those three things, whatever happens, it'll be the right thing.

Do you want to date the guy he had been before the can had been opened? Or the one afterwards, who knows himself? I'll have the worms, please.

For Helen, the value of having an emotionally enlightened ex and his big-hearted partner in her life has literally changed her life. She had been trying for almost a decade to have children. Various relationships had come and gone, but as she says: 'When you want to have children, you make very different choices about your relationships than you would if you didn't want to have children. My biological clock was literally thumping in my ear.'

So she approached an ex-boyfriend from university, who she had always stayed in touch with and remained fond of.

I found out I couldn't have children at all, so I also needed an egg donor. It seemed important to me that the sperm came from someone that I had actually slept with. He agreed to be a sperm donor and I became pregnant with twins. Obviously that all took a bit of time as it was all done through a clinic and there was a rigorous counselling process to go through.

While that was all happening, he met and fell in love with a woman who also had her own much older daughter. But because of complications in their relationship (she was married to someone else, so they spent quite a lot of time being on and off) he didn't tell her about the twins until quite a while after they had been born.

When they eventually got together and she found out about the twins, and me, she understandably felt uncertain about who I was and what the twins and I meant to him. Their dad and I were very close because we'd known each other so long, and it was hard for her to work out what our relationship was and how we all fitted together. So I went to see her without him, to reassure her, and we talked it all through, and then we all met the twins together, with her daughter there as well.

We're not the kind of people who would normally find each other; they are committed Buddhists and I work in the music industry; our worlds couldn't be further apart. And yet something has grown between us all that is really magic. Her daughter adores the twins, and they often go and stay there even if their dad isn't at home. I sometimes think the younger me would have really struggled to find the good in the situation and tried to keep the kids away from her. But because I was older, and had been through so much just to get them here, I've just always felt like the more people who can love them, the better. I got my friend back, and a new friend, and the children got a dad.

There have been wobbles. Once, quite early on, I found out that they had been swimming with her while their dad wasn't there. Part of me was incandescent. I couldn't believe that he had arranged for her to take them swimming without talking to me about it first (they were still quite young, and swimming was pretty major fun for them). But then I spoke to a friend about it and he said, 'You need to get out of your own way. Someone wants to take your kids swimming – enjoy it!'

Even when relationships don't last or turn into something bigger, there is a sense of single mothers feeling more empowered than their former selves and more inclined to establish boundaries. Rowan says:

> Having my daughter when I did, because I wanted to, it means I am expecting so much more for myself now. Before I had her I felt my desire to have children was really colouring my dating choices, but now I can really see people clearly and decide if I want them on my own terms. It works both ways as well, because it has really validated my choices for me, that going solo was the right thing to do.

I haven't found my second time around yet. I don't know at this point if I ever will. But that's okay. It always sounds a bit doth-protest-too-much when single women tell you how very happy they are to be single. We think they're just saying it and underneath it all they really just want to marry the handsome prince and live happily ever after like everyone else.

As Paul Dolan writes in *Happy Ever After*: 'It's as though the choice to be single is too great an affront on our collective ethics to have stemmed from a position of sincerity. It's almost a provocation.'[25]

But there is one big reason why single women are always telling you how much they love being single, and it is this: because it is the

---

25   Paul Dolan (2020) *Happy Ever After: A Radical New Approach to Living Well*. London: Penguin, page 76.

truth! Being single makes a lot of women very happy! How about we try believing them!

The Californian social scientist and professor of psychology Bella DePaulo has written extensively on the upsides of being single (i.e. not married or cohabiting) and the damaging myth that getting married makes us all happier.

Her TED talks, books and articles are bursting with detailed analyses of studies and research that – through my layperson's lens – all come to the same essential conclusion: that the fairytale of being married, which we are fed by popular culture every day, somehow makes anyone happier is still very much a fairytale. Being married, or living in a way that emulates a marriage, does not in fact improve anyone's life satisfaction, and the only people who get to live longer when they are married are men. For women, years of marriage and motherhood, with all their full-time caregiving and physical and emotional graft, are actually life-shortening. In fact Paul Dolan cites one Swiss study of 100,000 people in which the authors found that single women had a 1.71 year higher life expectancy, while men on average lived 1.54 years longer if they were married.[26] Being married actually makes men live longer and women die younger. No wonder women are happy when they're single; the alternative kills us. Where is this health warning when we walk up the aisle and promise to love and to cherish?

Single people, says DePaulo, embrace bigger, broader meanings of relationships and love. They develop better life skills and practical knowledge than their married/cohabiting counterparts. They care more about meaningful work and pursue opportunities to develop their passions. They are kinder, caring more for relatives and people who need them than married people, who DePaulo goes as far as

---

26 Paul Dolan (2020) *Happy Ever After: A Radical New Approach to Living Well*. London: Penguin, page 80.

to say can become 'greedy and insular', prioritising their marriage above everything and everyone else.

She also describes how it's difficult to accurately measure happiness in married/cohabiting versus divorced people because it's not as simple as putting people into two groups and asking them to tick a box. Some people might be depressed but married or cohabiting, or insanely happy and divorced. The next best thing, she says, is to track people over a period of time and measure their happiness according to their life stages. Discussing one such study, she says:

> It was the people who got divorced who felt worse at first, but then felt better and better over time. The people who used to be single and then got married, felt either a little bit better at first (or their feelings/appraisals did not change or they got a bit worse), and then, over time, their feelings/appraisals either stayed about the same or got worse over time. The timelines of wellbeing suggest that getting divorced makes you happier over time; and getting married does not make you happier, and may even make you less happy.[27]

I like DePaulo's exuberant defence of the single life and would urge everyone to read her research and watch her TED Talk: 'What no one ever told you about people who are single' and read her books *Singled Out* and *Alone: The Badass Psychology of People Who Like Being Alone.*[28]

But for me, the point is not about winning a happiness argument or proving that the smug-marrieds are wrong and the happy, kind singles are right; I know plenty of married people who are both happy and not remotely selfish. It's about normalising the idea that

27 Bella DePaulo, belladepaulo.com

28 Bella DePaulo (2017) *Alone: The Badass Psychology of People Who Like Being Alone.*

being single/divorced/dating/whatever you want to be at any point in your life can be a happy place, in and of itself. And it would be really helpful if everyone could stop assuming the opposite.

Because sometimes it's the not meeting the expectations of others around you that can be the hardest part of being single. It's hard to feel you are not up to the same scratch as everyone else, unable or unwilling to jump through the same hoops. I often wonder how these expectations actually affect my own self-perception. Would I be happier if everyone stopped expecting me to be miserable, or lacking somehow, because I'm single? It's another rabbit hole I don't need to get stuck down. And as any decent therapist will tell you: what other people think is, ultimately, their business and theirs alone. You can only be responsible for your own feelings and control the things that you can control. There is a great freedom in realising and accepting this truth.

The definition of insanity

'The definition of insanity is doing the same thing over and over and expecting different results.'

This famous quote is widely attributed to Albert Einstein, and plenty of single mothers have shared this eureka moment. Namely, the realisation that they don't need to get married and do the whole thing in the same way again to enjoy the rest of their lives and relationships with other people.

For many, especially if they have been through an expensive and complicated divorce, it's about keeping new situations simple.

'I am never putting myself through that again,' says Nikki.

> Not unless he is uber-rich and on death's door! Maybe if he kept his own place and I kept mine, for an easy escape. But I can't imagine ever putting myself in another situation that is so difficult to extricate myself from.

For others it's a fear of finding themselves returned to the realms of domesticity.

Claire says: 'The idea of remarrying isn't hugely appealing at this point in time as my independence is now fully resumed. The thought of having someone else relying on me again doesn't fill me with great joy.'

For some, the blending of families with children of different ages and the pressure of becoming a step-parent can be too much to cope with.

Diane's ex moved in with his girlfriend and her son during the lockdowns of 2020. She said:

> The kids hardly knew his girlfriend and found her son difficult at times, and of course it was a strange situation with a lot of fear around Covid, so they really kicked against it and basically refused to go to his new house for a long time. It put such a lot of pressure on all of us, it made me realise I wouldn't be moving anyone in here or living with someone else again, not until the children have left home anyway. It's too much to expect.

And for others, simply swearing off re-marriage isn't enough; it's about redefining the whole meaning of a relationship and what you want from it.

In 2020 ABC's comedy *Single Parents* ran a storyline about a polyamorous relationship between three of the show's characters (a 'throuple'). In this kind of ethical monogamy (not to be confused with polygamy, in which men simply collect wives, and threesomes, which is just the sex), consenting adults of all genders and sexual orientations can be in loving, committed and intimate relationships with three, sometimes four or five, or more, people.

This is not just a story for laughs on TV: the practice of polyamory is on the rise. At least it's on the rise in the very small proportion of mostly Western cultures where a monogamous relationship style has the majority rule. Some figures suggest around 80 per cent of the world's cultures permit polyamory, with people sharing a number of committed relationships and raising children as part of a group that is larger than our 2.4 family. The cultural explanations for this are complex but boil down largely to the explanation that we switched to monogamy in Victorian times, for the cost efficiencies, it being cheaper to keep one woman than three or four. Prostitutes, maids and other surplus women could fill the gaps, physically and metaphorically.

Today in the US it's estimated around 10–12 million adults are in polyamorous relationships, and around five per cent of ever-progressive Canadians now identify as poly – with half of them being parents.

I can see why polyamory is an attractive option, especially to younger single parents. The labour of raising a family is shared, not only with one other partner but a whole bunch of other adults who you like and trust. You're not alone, but you're not a spouse or a partner either. You get real downtime, and you can play to your strengths as a parent instead of being a frazzled everymum. Childcare isn't a problem and nor is getting a babysitter.

When you consider my own parents' backstory and just how rife adultery is in monogamous cultures – in a government survey reported on by *The Sun* newspaper,[29] one in five British adults admitted to having had an affair, and of those who have had an affair, only half had stopped at one; twenty per cent had three or more and eight per cent had five or more, and these are the just the people who admitted it – you begin to wonder if polyamory is such a strange thing after all. Maybe adultery is simply the natural

---

29 1 in 5 British adults says they've had an affair. https://yougov.co.uk/topics/ lifestyle/articles-reports/2015/05/27/one-five-british-adults-admit-affair

human instinct to share more than one intimate adult relationship, manifesting regardless in a culture that still labels it a sin.

It's not for me though. I can barely muster the enthusiasm for one relationship, let alone five. Besides, how do you even go about starting that kind of relationship? I will leave that to the Millennials and Gen-Z'ers. And plenty of single mothers are in the same emotional boat, with many making the 'single life' a way of life.

Call it celibacy, call it self-partnering, or plain old being single – single mothers are embracing the freedoms of a life without permanent significant attachments. Not only because 'freedom' makes life so much, well, freer, and not because they are all hideously unattractive or what the patriarchy likes to call 'difficult women'. But because it allows them a level of authenticity and self-acceptance they haven't experienced before.

As Deborah Levy writes in her memoir *The Cost of Living*:

> Neo-patriarchy required us to be passive but ambitious, maternal but erotically energetic, self-sacrificing but fulfilled – we were to be Strong Modern Women, while being subjected to all kinds of humiliations both economic and domestic. If we felt guilty about everything most of the time, we were not sure what it was we had actually done wrong.[30]

For an increasing number of single mothers, freedom from the expectations of the patriarchy – that feeling of having done something wrong, of not being enough – affords a new, albeit unfamiliar feeling of contentment. Unfamiliar because we are taught to run away from it from the moment we are born, but contentment none the less.

---

30 Deborah Levy (2019) *The Cost of Living*. London: Penguin.

Hey there, lonely girl

Don't you get lonely? My mum asks me this from time to time, usually when there is no love-interest on the scene. Of course I get lonely. I am not an automaton, even if I find 'feelings' easier to live without at times. When I am not seeing anyone, and all my friends are busy and my children only want me for money and food, I feel moments of loneliness. It is most noticeable in the mornings, or when I am ill, when there is no one to bring me a cup of tea in bed. That was a nice thing about being married – someone made me a cup of tea. As a single mother I have to enter into major negotiations with teenagers, usually shouting our terms through the walls, in order to receive a warm beverage in my chamber (which is often only lukewarm and made with the wrong tea bags, so that I get a kind of peppermint cream drink, rather than the hot mug of builders' I'm really craving). Then, and when I'm asked to write down my next of kin on a form, there is something a bit tragic about writing my sister's name and not the name of a man who will come crashing through the doors on his horse when I need the kind of next-of-kin rescue I'm writing their name down for.

But these are fleeting moments. I've realised that they are very often down to self-pity rather than true loneliness. And other people's expectations. Recently, at a party, someone asked me: 'So when did your husband leave?' as though it was a given that I had been deserted. Another time, when a friend spotted me holding hands with my boyfriend in the street, she texted me to say: 'It's great to see you happy' as though when I walk along unattached to a man, I am automatically a vision of misery. And when I took my children out for dinner to celebrate my birthday, we sat down at the table and looked at our menus, and we kept on looking, and looking. And after a while I thought it was taking a long time for the waiter to come, so I caught their eye, gesturing that we'd like to order. 'Oh, sorry!' she said. 'I thought you were waiting for someone else to arrive!'

I also find it useful to remember that relationships and marriages can be very lonely places indeed. Feeling misunderstood, underappreciated and generally unloved is not the sole territory of single women. In fact I'd argue that the loneliness is amplified when you are living next to someone who, for whatever reason, doesn't get you. Or perhaps it's that they get you so much that they actually dislike you.

'I hate you and everything you stand for' one friend's husband said to her recently. It reminded me of the nasty notes Antony Armstrong-Jones was said to leave hidden for Princess Margaret to find in her drawers, sequestered in her gloves and lingerie. One was a list entitled 24 Things I Hate About You. Another read: ' You look like a Jewish manicurist and I hate you.' As my favourite band Erasure once sang: who needs love like that? Of course, not every marriage is so spiteful. But I know that simply by not being married, a bunch of negative, unhappy feelings and emotions – everything from suspicion and jealousy to resentment and pity – do not feature in my life as much, if at all, as they did when I was married. The idea that a marriage is some kind of emotional Shangri-La where you never feel bad things or alone is another part of the fantasy.

Says Bella DePaulo:

> …there is no good evidence that getting married makes people less lonely. In fact, in some suggestive research, strikingly low rates of loneliness were found among the people we expect, stereotypically, to be the loneliest: older women who have always been single.[31]

---

31 Bella DePaulo, belladepaulo.com

All about attachment

Being single, and sometimes not single, as a mother has certainly prompted some self-reflection and investigation for me that I might never have explored had I stayed married. I have read more books and followed more Instagram accounts on the subject than is necessary, but none has been quite so impactful and so helpful in understanding *everything* as Amir Levine's *Attached*.[32]

Attachment theory was first formulated by the British psychologist John Bowlby in 1958. Bowlby identified the correlation between a child's relationship with their primary caregiver (most often their mother) and their own psychological development. Observing orphans in a London home, he realised that without the safety and reassurance of that one strong bond with a responsive parent or other figure, children went on to experience greater difficulties and 'maladjustments' in life.

Fifty years later, the Canadian psychiatrist and neuroscientist Amir Levine took Bowlby's theory of attachment and applied it to adult relationships, suggesting that the way we received care and love from our primary carers in infancy is a blueprint for the way we receive care and love in our adult relationships.

Levine identifies three main styles of attachment – the way we relate to our adult relationships: anxious, avoidant and secure. Clearly this is a simplified synopsis of the attachment styles, but it goes something like this:

- Anxiously attached people are, as their name suggests, uncertain and preoccupied in their relationships and require

32 Dr Amir Levine and Rachel S.F. Heller (2019) *Attached: Are You Anxious, Avoidant or Secure? How the Science of Adult Attachment Can Help You Find – and Keep – Love.* London: Bluebird.

constant reassurance from their partners and generally live in fear of being abandoned.

- Avoidants also fear abandonment and loss but deal with it by avoiding intimacy and closeness. They can be extraordinarily independent and uncomfortable with being vulnerable, seeing emotional dependency as weak or needy.
- Securely attached people are warm and loving, comfortable with closeness and do not fear intimacy or being vulnerable. The sun shines on securely attached people.

There are no prizes for guessing who we should all try to be in a relationship with. But Levine breaks the sad news that you won't find many people with a secure attachment style in the dating pool, because – irony of ironies – they're all already in secure and loving relationships! Or, another way of saying it: all the good ones are taken.

Instead, says Levine, the dating pool is awash with avoidant and anxiously attached people. Who, it will come as no surprise to hear, generally make a terrible match. As one pushes towards, the other pulls away, and vice versa. It all makes such a lot of sense. Understanding attachment styles in romantic relationships has been one of the biggest light-bulb moments of my single-mother experience.

Although after my initial delight at finally feeling like I understood the rules and why perhaps I hadn't yet met Mr Right, or even Mr Vaguely Suitable, I realised that it meant me too. I did the quiz in the back of the book, and realised I am an anxious-avoidant. The terrible hybrid-mutant-child of the anxious and avoidant attachment styles. The kind of royal pain in the arse who thinks you don't love her if you don't reply to her text message but also immediately dumps you if you show her the slightest hint of affection.

Oh dear.

Still, seeing my relationships through the prism of attachment theory has helped me understand things better and helped me to be kinder to myself about why things hadn't yet 'worked out' with anyone – if working out is still something we measure in units of time, like endurance races and prison sentences. Understanding my attachment style means I no longer see myself as lucky, or unlucky, in love; I have simply been behaving according to my attachment style and the things that happen when my attachment style meets another attachment style.

The good news, says Levine, is that attachment styles are fluid, so that you are not simply a prisoner in your own attachment style forever. It's not your personality and it's not a lifetime diagnosis. It's a way of relating to others we have learned in childhood. It's not always easy to break habits of a lifetime, but it's not impossible. I'd say that as I write this (and partly as a result of writing this), I am doing the work to become a securely attached person. And in the meantime, anxious or avoidants, or those of us who are both, can get more from their experiences simply by being aware of their attachment styles. Where once I might have seen an emotionally unavailable man as some kind of personal challenge, I now know that this is my attachment style in action, and I can walk away from it (him) before disaster strikes. That's the theory, anyway…

Doing things differently

As time has passed the idea of settling down again or finding another 'the one' seems to feel less and less important to me. And I find myself wondering if, despite my *horreur* at my mother's question of who would want me with two children, it has in fact been me who has been thinking in old money all this time. Trying to replace like for like?

Feeling more content in my own company, enjoying that of my friends so much, sometimes dating, sometimes not dating, I have learned to self-soothe in times of loneliness and – although not always – to be more discerning in my choices. My brother-in-law describes me as being 'picky, but in a good way'. I am happy with this description. And yet a small part of me still feels I'm not supposed to feel like that; I'm supposed to want to marry the prince. The fairytale is potent. And so I still find the conflicting agendas that live inside my head and heart to be confusing and uncomfortable at times. And I worry that I sound perhaps a little bit burdensome and entitled. Am I still just being that difficult child who refuses to go to bed? And I have to remind myself: a man would be highly unlikely to find this description anything to worry about.

With this emotional armour on board it does become easier to see relationships on their own terms. Ideas of something being 'successful' only if it lasts forever, and that dreadful phrase 'the breakdown of a relationship', have both come to feel increasingly irrelevant. What if there is no success or failure in relationships, there are simply relationships that are good and others that are less good? Some last a long time, others burst almost immediately; none has more or less value than the other. What if marriages don't break down, they just expire sometimes? What if monogamy with one person forevermore is something I'm just not built for? After all, lifetime monogamy, where partners choose to have sex with only one person for their whole life, only occurs as the norm in one other species on the entire planet: owl monkeys. Maybe I just don't have a lot of owl monkey in my genes.

Swiping through the endless bad selfies and photos of men holding fish on dating apps, I find I am less inclined these days to linger over the 'right' choices or to swipe right on the doctors and the lawyers and the men who have children the same age as mine, because that might make things easier when we all get married and live happily ever after. Instead I'm more influenced by simple chemistry: a face I like, a funny turn of phrase. Removing all of the pressure to find 'success' or a new happy ending opens up a whole new way of being. I'm not failing and I'm not succeeding. I'm just here, experiencing. It's a kind of relationship mindfulness that, much like any kind of mindfulness, I don't always manage to get right. But when I do, I take a deep breath, enjoy the moment and try not to worry about the past or the future.

A few thoughts on dating, from one single mother to another

On becoming Bertha Mason

In the eight years I've been dating, I have rarely heard a man say a nice thing about his ex-wife. I have heard a lot of them described as 'bipolar' (this seems to be the pop-psyche diagnosis du jour for women who men can't have sex with any more, but who they also have to give money to), toxic, mental, manipulative, conniving and warped. The nation is infested with emotionally unstable ex-wives according to their ex-husbands. We are all Bertha Mason – the psychotic ex-wife in Charlotte Brontë's *Jane Eyre*, who Mr Rochester keeps locked in his attic: an insane albatross around a good man's neck.

'Never marry a man you wouldn't want to be divorced from,' said Nora Ephron, in her collection of essays *I Feel Bad About My Neck*.[33] I concur. The way a man talks about his ex-wife tells you pretty much everything you need to know about him. Ask about a man's relationship with his ex-wife early on, and if any of the above words are mentioned run for the hills.

---

33 Nora Ephron (2008) *I Feel Bad About My Neck: And Other Thoughts on Being a Woman.* London: Transworld.

Get real

Opinion is divided on this as I know some people like being able to 'warm up' with cyber-chat before meeting in real life. But I've learned that it is all too easy to idealise someone on WhatsApp, only to find they have really hairy earlobes that make you feel queasy in real life. There is no replacement for that first impression in real life. If you can find time to meet for a coffee asap, you will save yourself a lot of wasted time if you don't connect.

Learn your attachment style

Understanding attachment styles and how yours can interact with a potential suitor's will be extremely useful, although I've yet to meet a man in dating land who knows about attachment styles. It's all a bit too much like star signs for them, I think. Coming at them with your attachment style quiz and a pen might not be a good look for a first date either. But even just approaching situations with attachment theory in mind can help, kind of like putting on a pair of glasses that bring everything into focus.

To meet or not to meet?

You don't introduce your partner to your children too soon because they will become attached and should the partner disappear from their lives, that will not be nice for them. Also, it will put your new partner off you. Under patriarchal dating rules, it is a woman's job to lure her man into commitment, to catch that guy with all her womanly powers. A couple of kids picking their noses at the dinner table will not help her cause.

In what other adult relationships do we practise this kind of ridiculous behaviour? When we meet a new friend, do we keep them from meeting our children until they are ready? Quite the opposite; most of us actively want our children to meet new people and have new experiences.

I mean, obviously, don't move him in after a month and make everyone start calling him Dad – that would be weird. But letting your children know you are a grown woman who enjoys the equal and entertaining company of a kind man or woman? And letting your new squeeze know you've got some cracking kids? There is only one system in which this might be a problem and it begins with P. People come and go in life. Showing them that relationships can and do expire seems like a wiser move than setting them up to believe in the myth of forever.

Rowan, a single mother by choice whose daughter is three, says:

> I've just started seeing someone more seriously and he is coming to stay at the weekend. He's going to stay in my room because I don't want to hide anything from her or let her think it's anything to be ashamed of. I'm just going to say he's my special friend and that special friends can have sleepovers sometimes. Why would I hide it?

Dating tips for single mums from love, sex and relationships coach Julia Kotziamani

Dating can make a huge difference to your mental and physical wellbeing and have a positive ripple effect on your family. But it can also be daunting, especially if you are just coming back into the world of intimacy after a long time away. Here are some tips for making it a more enjoyable, expansive and exciting experience.

1. Make sure the practical elements are taken care of

There is nothing more stressful than worrying about your children when trying to get to know someone on a date. Make sure you have competent childcare you trust and easy access to checking in. For some this means organising childcare that is not their co-parent. Knowing that this is totally taken care of means you're not in two places at once, mentally.

2. Take the pressure off

First dates are an opportunity to see if you want another drink/ coffee with someone, they are not where we assess how good a life partner or step-parent someone might be. Do I feel comfortable? Am I enjoying myself? Am I attracted to this person? These are the early date questions you should be asking yourself, not whether or not they will be an amazing co-parent.

Rushing too far ahead will stop you from giving great people a chance and prevent you from being in touch with how you are feeling in this person's company. It can also make you overlook really important red flags, especially if you have a history of attraction to abusive partners.

3. Practise until it's easy

Flirting, great conversation, seduction are all buildable skills you can learn. If you don't feel they come naturally to you, then remember it's the same for lots of us and you can develop these skills with practice. Give yourself time and grace to make mistakes and learn from them, especially if it's been a while.

4. Know your patterns and break your own rules

Women face a daily onslaught of how relationships ought to look, and how we can hope to find them. Even the smartest, most savvy among us will be affected by this narrative at some level. Typically women are meant to be passive, and to work on being 'chosen'. Add all our experiences, attachment styles and personal preferences, and it is hard for any of us to reach adulthood with a romantic clean slate. And having children does not stop us repeating mistakes that don't serve us.

Take the time to really understand yourself and your own history. From there you can decide which rules you want to take forward. Becoming a parent is a great time to have a forensic look at the landscape of your desires and rewrite things that will no longer suit or serve you. As parents, there is so much pressure to 'get it right'. When you take that stress away your love and sex lives can go through an incredible revolution. When we start learning what works for us, we can build really beautiful dynamics that are much more fulfilling for us, and in turn for our families as well.

5. Know you have more options than you think

One of my favourite go-to sayings is f*ck the fairytale! There is so much freedom and fun to be had in realising that you get to write your own rules. Want to go celibate for a year and get to know yourself and your body much better? Go for it. Want to seek a new spouse to have more kids with? Great. Want to spend all your child-free nights engaging in the delicious, decadent orgies of your wildest fantasies? Super! Want to try dating different genders, numbers of partners, 'types' than before? Fantastic! As with all elements of being a solo parent, you get to make the rules and that's something to celebrate.

6. Rejection is inevitable

We all get rejected at some point. Relationships involving other people are only ever partially in our control, and though we can and should take full responsibility for the part we play in them, we are not going to be what everyone is looking for every time. That is fine. Rejection is not a reflection of your worth or value as a person. When you manage to separate your self-worth from what people think of you, dating becomes much more light-hearted and fun.

7. Understand what you are up against and bend it to your will

Dating is inherently sexist. Single mums are demonised in a way that single dads simply are not. Single mums face stigma that single women do not. People will judge and blame you for what has happened in your life, and some will expect you to accept scraps. Do not accept scraps. Now is the time to raise, not lower, your standards. It sounds cliche but know your worth. If you struggle with self-esteem, write a list of all the attractive qualities you have gained as a result of becoming a mum. Maybe you are more empathetic and caring, maybe you run a household that is glorious fun to live in, maybe you have a new fire in your heart or have grown in resilience and passion. Maybe it's as simple as acquiring some new curves. Do this and watch your confidence grow.

8. Get back your spark

To enjoy dating, we must find our more sensual personas. The key to any great date is being confident enough with yourself not to feel self-conscious. When we are too self-conscious it's very hard to be present and even harder to work out whether we actually like the person in front of us. Sex appeal is about feeling good about yourself, and it is not easy to develop unshakable self-love. Some of us must instead aim for some self-acceptance first. The key is to stop comparing yourself to anyone else. You are you, now, and that is beautiful. Your life has led you here, and you carry the wisdom, values and body you have gained. Now is the time to work with yourself where you are, and on knowing in your deepest core that you are worthy of love, respect and deep, passionate pleasure.

There are loads of ways to start tuning back in to your more decadent side, but the first is to give yourself permission to experience pleasure on a daily basis. This can be as small as choosing what you really want for dinner and savouring it, or wearing clothes that feel divine on your skin. Take this slowly and at a pace that doesn't trigger you, as this is an area where lots of us hold trauma. You can work up to full afternoons of masturbation and intense, mind-blowing, self-delivered orgasms. The more pleasure you give yourself, the more sex appeal you will ooze, and the more confident you will be receiving pleasure from others.

9. Stay safe

No meeting strangers in private places, always practise safe sex, and don't put yourself in situations where you feel unsafe. It is so important to make sure you dive into new romance at a pace you are comfortable with, and if you have a history of abuse or fears around new people, then slow it right down to suit you. Dating needs to be fun, playful and exciting, and this is not compatible with fear. Dating also doesn't have to look like anything in particular. Breakfasts, coffees and walks in public places are great first-date options, so don't just rely on late-night drinks. Anyone worth their salt will respect this. As always, removing the sources of stress will give you room for clarity on whether you are actually attracted to the person you are with and makes dating way, way more fun.

CHAPTER FIVE

How Will You Live?

You've always been crazy, this is just the first chance
you've had to express yourself.
Louise Sawyer, *Thelma and Louise*

Sundays were the hardest day. Sundays when we were all living together had always been about making lunch, walking the dog, seeing our families. We watched family movies on Sundays, did DIY and pottered around in the garden. These traditional Sunday activities were the evidence that we were a normal family. On the other days of the week we were bots in a video game, moving in and out of the house, bumping into walls, blasting commands at each other, exploding. On Sundays we moved as one. On Sundays there was time.

And it was all that time that made those first Sundays as separate units so hard. If the children were at home and it was just the three of us, I was faced with a long, adult-less day, unpunctuated by activities or commitments or grown-up conversation. I felt their father's absence on those Sundays and grieved for what had been lost. What were we supposed to do on Sundays without him around? Everyone else was spending time with their own families, doing their family things, and I wasn't yet feeling inclined to host convivial Sunday lunches by myself. We live in a small rural town, so art galleries and shopping centres and other urban things-to-do were not an option for us. We were lucky if the supermarket was open. Instead we had the beach and the countryside, expansive picture-perfect landscapes all around us that other people visited on their holidays. But the eyes get blurry when the spirit is low. When the children moaned about going on another walk I didn't push it. I didn't want to go on another walk either. They watched films and YouTube, and I emptied cupboards and rearranged sock drawers, all the while feeling certain I was the only woman in the world who was not having a lovely, stylish, papers-and-kids-in-bed Sunday.

Waking up to an empty house on a Sunday wasn't any better. For me one of the greatest paradoxes of motherhood has always been the way I long for time to myself, only to miss my children like the proverbial amputated limb when they aren't nearby. Now, when they were spending time with their father, which was absolutely what they should have been doing, I had no option but to suck it up. I couldn't tune in to their chit chat from another room just so I could hear their voices, or peek in on them playing. I couldn't come home early or decide on a whim to do something with them. (They were too young to have phones, and even now I try not to text them when they are in their other life, with him. I've spent enough time in the company of single fathers whose exes text their children, trying to stay 'involved' from a distance, to know that it doesn't usually help.) They were no longer mine, on those Sundays. And everyone we knew was still spending time with their own families, and the small rural town was still quiet and empty. I still didn't want to go for another walk. I emptied more cupboards and rearranged rooms, washed school uniforms and prepared for their return.

And I worked. The burden of caring for children falls more heavily on women and means women are more likely to suffer 'workplace disadvantages' as a result. Every working mother I've ever met has known this all along, but it was only in June 2021 that an Employment Appeal Tribunal in England finally established this as a legal precedent. Nurse and mother of three Gemma Dobson brought the appeal after being sacked when she refused to sign a new 'flexible hours' contract that would have made it impossible for her to juggle childcare with ever-changing shift patterns. The case meant that it could now be taken as read that the 'childcare disparity' means women shoulder more of the caring burden than men. Only a couple of thousand years too late guys but hey, praise be.

I couldn't work in the straight nine-to-five way their father did, not because I was lying around eating Wagon Wheels and watching *Trisha* as it sometimes felt that I had to make clear, but because as their mother large parts of my day were/are taken up not necessarily with physical childcare – no one needed their nappies changing or books being read to them any more – but with the secondary childcare jobs. Washing their clothes, cleaning their rooms, filling out forms for school trips, shopping for school lunches, cooking dinner, arranging play dates, hosting play dates, booking dental appointments, arranging birthday parties and generally being a roadie for the stars of the show. As a roadie I would be paid for delivering all of this of course. But as a mum, less so. Get your domestic load cheap at half the price.

My self-employment, as a copywriter at that stage, had always worked for us as a family because I could work around my other job, as a mother. That's the public face of being self-employed: the fabled flexibility. But in reality it meant that when the children were with their dad I worked. (I'm actually writing this now, on a Saturday, while the children are at their dad's.) Because there are often not enough hours in the week to do a full-time job and be a full-time roadie and a full-time chatelaine, even if your chateaux is a small mid-terrace ex-council.

As with the money, I raged about this imbalance. Sometimes privately, a lot of the time to him, who at times I know I have blamed for the patriarchy's entire playbook. But I knew it wasn't his fault, or anyone's apart from my own. And fault wasn't the right word, either. It was simply the way it had always been, or rather how it had become. As divorce lawyer Claire Costley puts it:

> It's very hard for a dysfunctional marriage to become a fully cooperative co-parenting team overnight.
>
> A lot of the fathers I meet get a shock because their working life has always been structured in a way that means they see their children in a more incidental sense: cleaning their teeth in the morning or dropping them off to football practice. They haven't always had to make the time for their children in the way the mothers have. When they realise that they will have to leave work early or arrange the childcare or be in for the Ocado delivery or whatever it is, they begin to kick back and don't necessarily want to share everything 50/50.
>
> Conversely, a lot of the mothers find it very difficult to 'let go' of their children every other weekend or whatever the arrangements are. They struggle to settle into these periods of time they have for themselves and often find it difficult to imagine a new life, or believe that they could enjoy a different way of life, and of being a mother.

It was true, I had spent so long being someone to other people – friend, girlfriend, sister, daughter, wife and mother – that I had entirely forgotten, or possibly never even learned, how to be myself. By myself. Those early Sundays alone exposed this missing part of me, the vital keystone that was supposed to hold it all together but had somehow never been put in place. I urgently needed to find it so that all the other pieces wouldn't collapse and kill everyone underneath me.

It took me a while.

My initial coping strategy for those uncomfortable weekends, once the work was done, was to go out. To partay. I was a free woman, and I was going to go out and have me some fun, find me some handsome dudes. As Rita, the sexually frustrated mother, says in the 2011 comedy *Bridesmaids*, when trying to persuade her peers that Las Vegas is a better option for the bachelorette party than a cosy lakeside cabin: 'I want balls in my face. Balls!'

But this was a strange thing, too. Going out by myself, or rather as a single woman with my friends (I hadn't yet turned to propping up the bar on my own of a Saturday, although these days I would see nothing wrong with it), without a husband's arm to be on, I felt oddly vulnerable. A feeling I just hadn't expected to experience.

My social life as a married woman had mostly been about dinner parties. We'd take the kids to a friend's house and let them run wild while all the grown-ups got steaming in the kitchen and smoked secret rollies in the garden. Once, with a family we saw a lot of when the children were small, we all got so drunk that we tried to hide in their kitchen cupboard to see if our children would notice. Six adults all trying to squeeze themselves in with the vacuum and the broom. I can still remember the children's faces when they found us and saw what we were doing. They were too young to swear but they were definitely thinking: *dickheads.*

I liked entertaining when I was married. It made me feel like I was getting it right. Some of my fondest childhood memories are of my parents' dining room on Friday nights, the candlelit room full of shoulder pads and slacks, the smell of Poison, and After Eights yet to be discovered in their little black packets. I liked recreating that scene in my home, everyone jolly and replete at my table. Or did I just like pleasing everyone and imagining what they might say when they got home? *Such a great night. Food was amazing. We must get them over soon.* Was it really just a way of proving my feminine worth in our small, local marketplace?

The dinner parties stopped as soon as we separated. I don't think I have been to one, at least not with any of the same people, since. Not when the men are there anyway. I have been on girls' nights out and for coffees and walks with some of the women in that group. But the dinner party circuit very quickly became a memory.

Naomi says the same thing happened when she and her ex split:

> I was really shocked by how the invites just suddenly dried up! We had always loved having people over and as a couple were great hosts. I couldn't believe how overnight I just wasn't on the 'couples dining' list any more. Friends want to meet me for lunch or a walk or whatever, but it's not the same. I say to them, no! I want to come for dinner and flirt with your husband!

I could pretend to be affronted, but I'm not. These gatherings are, after all, based on unspoken rules of extreme gender archetyping. Rules so unspoken that no one knew they existed until one of us broke them. These gatherings were for husbands and wives. It was an even-numbers-only club, and I had chosen to no longer wear the tie.

I don't think anyone truly saw me as competition. And yet I know it would have been awkward to go to a dinner party with the people who really only knew me as part of a couple. Women who knew me in my relation to him and whose conversations were in relation to theirs and their families. And of course even just inviting me would have meant a perceived allegiance to my 'side' because in the old patriarchal narrative, divorce is a great feud and sides must be picked and stakes claimed early on. Although at times I felt sad about it, I did understand why that era had to come to an end. No tie, no entry.

So, if I could find a friend who wasn't at a dinner party, I went out. And it felt different. Nights out and shenanigans had been a feature of my life since my teens. Socialising had always been a large part of who I was. In one marriage counselling session I was described by the other party as being 'too sociable'. The psychology of how and why that became true was probably all part of the same end-of-the-road problem.

But I was older now. And I had never lived alone like this before. I'd always shared taxis home with someone, eaten cheese on toast with someone, unpicked the hazy memories and mortified recollections of the night before in fits of giggles with a real-life human. These moments of camaraderie were as much a part of the fun as the night itself. Now I walked home alone. Once, I lost my keys on the way home and I had to wake up my elderly neighbours at three o'clock in the morning – sweet, lovely people; their grandson was in my son's class – to get my spare from them. Forty-two years old, swaying in my neighbours' kitchen at three in the morning. My old friends and I have always called the remorse experienced with a particularly bad hangover 'The Badgers': the anthropomorphization of our demons, albeit in badger form, has always seemed somehow to lessen the grip of our self-loathing. I woke up with a whole cete of badgers the day after that episode. I woke up with them quite a lot when my children weren't nearby.

Over time the need to fill my empty spaces with hedonism receded, and I learned to sit more comfortably with the silence. Staying in on a Saturday night alone slowly became less scary, partly because I began online dating, which felt like being in a virtual nightclub from morning to night, to begin with at least. But also because I began to feel at home with myself and my own company. People tell you everything is a phase when your children are small. This is also true when you're a fledgling single mother.

I have learned to entertain again, but in a different way. Impromptu, with friends, usually according to who has their children, or a night off. Casual plates of quickly knocked-up food and shop-bought puddings, watching a film. Take-aways and, best of all, eating out. Not really entertaining at all, if I'm honest. Without any husbands around I no longer feel I need to put on that show. I take part in and enjoy the experience so much more this way and grieve a little for all the years I spent my Saturdays making curry pastes from scratch.

Dinner parties weren't the only thing that stopped. Moaning: I stopped moaning so much. As a married woman I had become a dreadful moaner. I moaned about all the usual household stuff that wives moan about – the socks left on the floor, the toothpaste lids, the bins. I moaned about the unfairness, the lack of communication, our never-the-twain approaches to parenting. And I moaned a lot about him; I became riddled with that particular kind of irritation that comes from spending too much time in close proximity to a person. The way he ate and the way he breathed, the weight of his footsteps and how they resonated through the floorboards, a sound that seemed to have been calculated specifically to piss me off. The poor guy couldn't open his eyes in the morning without me finding something to criticise and moan about. I could write a whole chapter on the moaning alone. When he came back from the supermarket one day with the wrong kind of broccoli and I really let him have it, I knew things had gotten out of hand.

Beneath every behaviour is a feeling and beneath that feeling a need. We do it from the moment we are born; we cry because we are cold or hungry or lonely and someone comes to soothe us. Only when we become adults, especially female ones, it's labelled nagging and we're told we're martyrs and ungrateful harridans. I moaned because I was unhappy, and I needed something to change. If you re-imagine the stereotype of a nagging wife as a woman who is simply letting it be known she is unhappy, think of all the unhappy wives there are in the world. The trouble-and-strife trope becomes the biggest gaslight of all time.

The relationship charity Relate published research in January 2019 that showed over a fifth of UK couples live in a 'distressed relationship' with the main reasons for staying together being for the sake of the kids, and the hope it will get better. Anecdotally, I'd say its way more than a fifth, but then maybe I only hang out with distressed people. Either way, so many married/cohabiting friends seem to exist in a state of low-level moaning. Their partner doesn't know them, they don't have anything to say to each other, they haven't had sex for months, sometimes years. They don't have shared interests, he is insular and miserable, he has no friends, if it wasn't for her they'd have no social life. He is selfish, he doesn't make time for the children, he has no idea how hard it is. She loves it when he is away. When she goes away, he just goes to his mum's. It all seems so much louder, and so unnecessary, now I don't need to do it.

It had been a heavy load, all that moaning. Realising it had gone felt like lifting the lap bar up after a particularly nauseating and unsafe theme-park ride.

I stopped going to the supermarket so much. Or maybe it was just that I spent less time there overall. Either way, my aisle-miles plummeted. I stopped doing those mindless 'big shops' with bumper packs of toilet rolls and baked beans on offer. I don't know why; it was only one fewer person to feed, and yet the need to churn out a meat-and-two-veg dinner every night left me, and with it went the pound coins and the big trolleys. In came baskets and quick nips around. We ate more simple, quick suppers: nice things on toast, frittatas and tray bakes; in fact anything that only used one pan and could still pass as healthy. I became good at making things we could all pick up with our hands that required no cutlery and therefore less washing up – fish finger sandwiches (the fancy kind, in pitta breads with lettuce and lemon juice), chicken fajitas, ploughman's style bread boards full of things to graze on, falafels. Dinner became an all-day brunch menu. I don't think I have batch cooked a thing since we split up. The freezer is full of fruit for smoothies now, another winning breakfast that requires no thought or preparation beyond pouring things into a blender.

I should make it clear that I had never been forced to put dinner on the table; he wasn't sitting there with his napkin around his neck and his knife and fork in his fists, waiting for me to feed him, although the cooking had always fallen to me somehow. And yet without a man in the house to feed – with that simple subtraction – I felt freer to make meals that made life easier. I completely stopped worrying about what to make for tea, and shopping. Another ride, another lap bar lifted.

I wouldn't say I stopped being house proud so much as I had to let it go. Moaning about the state of the house and how much more of the housework I did than him, and then doing more of it to prove my righteous point, had become our normal. No one has ever accused me of being a clean-freak or uncommonly tidy, but over the years we had established certain ground rules to keep 'on top' of the house. We cleared up at night so the kitchen was clear-ish in the morning, tried to make the hallway clear before we left the house so we weren't greeted with mess when we returned. I always made the bed in the morning and put the pointless cushions on so it would look inviting later on when it was time to crawl back into it. Nothing you could describe as OCD, but a few familiar ways, the overall aim being that I could sit down at the end of the day and watch something on telly with a glass of wine the size of my head in my hand and feel I was entitled to do so. That was all.

(This Nirvana was rarely reached because I worked from home all day at that point and could therefore always find some housework that needed to be done, as well as some paid work that wasn't getting done, winding myself up into a frenzy of work/life imbalance that seemed to peak around the time he got home. He was tired and seeking sustenance and rest just at the time I wanted an extra pair of hands to get me through the next few hours. I remember a friend burst out laughing at me when I complained very seriously to her: 'The problem is he thinks home is somewhere for him to relax in!')

It all stopped, what orderliness there had been. It disappeared under a pile of laundry. There is a popular image of single mothers as slatterns and I'm sure on some days my house looks pretty neglected. It's not an intentional neglect: it's not a characteristic of the breed to live in chaos, it's just that one person can only do so much, especially when she is under constant fire from two children who don't yet know how to close the fridge, only how to open it. I've had to learn to leave it all behind me and shut the door, to anticipate the mess when I come home so that it doesn't make my heart sink quite so much when I walk in. And I've had to come to see the mess not as mess but as work in progress. It is jobs I haven't finished yet. Some I haven't started. Besides, would a single dad be worried about the state of his house? The few whose houses I've spent time in certainly haven't been. They call their houses bachelor pads and celebrate their mess and the freedom from their former life – the old ball and chain – that it represents. Either that or they don't notice it at all. The state of some of their shower mats, honestly. But surely there is something to learn from that.

I also had to start doing more of what one friend refers to as 'blue jobs' for myself. I had never been the kind of wife who believed she shouldn't have to put the bins out or felt there were tasks only my husband was capable of because of his Y chromosome. I remember him coming home one day aghast to find me eight months pregnant, standing on a stool painting the kitchen cupboards. And yet somehow, I had become the cook and the washer woman, and he did indeed put the bins out, do all the handiwork and all the car maintenance. Tempting as it was to still call him every time I needed someone to fix a door knob, I knew I had to pick up some of these jobs for myself. Not the big jobs. I paid – still pay – other men to put in cupboards and hang heavy things. I did do a one-day DIY course and learned how to use a drill, but I am still slightly terrified of it and what it might do in the wrong hands (mine). But the smaller jobs. Changing lightbulbs, putting air in the tyres, bleeding radiators, decorating, assembling flatpack, moving furniture, hanging things, putting up the tent, buying the Christmas tree, dealing with power cuts and broken boilers and WiFi and yes – putting the bins out. I have never really stopped and savoured the sense of independence and self-reliance these tasks tend to come with – they are not especially fun, there's a reason it's called Do It Yourself – and yet they are greater than the sum of their parts. My children see me do these things. They can barely remember a time when their mum didn't put the bins out. And I always allow myself a wry smile when married friends complain about jobs not being done, or the unfairness of their load. I am exhausted, it's true, but I am also free from the narrative that someone else is responsible or isn't pulling their weight. Having no one else to blame but yourself is not always such a bad thing.

These were not big, radical changes to my life. I still did the same job, lived in the same house, ploughed practically all of the same furrows. I didn't retrain as a cranial osteopath or sign myself up for a Tough Mudder. I didn't cut off all my hair or get a tattoo or do anything different much with the way I looked, although I did lose a lot of weight at the start, a result of only eating avocados and wine and other things that did not require preparation or washing up. And the tattoo idea lingers. Something about making that mark on my body appeals now in a way it never has before. They say that tattoos are the scars you choose, after all.

Rebecca Vincent is a tattoo artist based in Hackney:

> Tattooing used to be mostly for young people, but over the past few years I've noticed more and more women in their 40s and 50s are coming to me after a divorce or a relationship ends or there's some other big change. It's about reclaiming themselves, doing something that is purely for them. I specialise in botanical and floral tattoos, so often the design will have a meaning behind it; maybe it's a birth flower or from a certain time of year. It might represent someone or a new beginning.
>
> I do a lot of first-time tattoos and, for so many of my customers, the tattoo is only part of the process. The whole experience is cathartic; they come and tell me everything. Lots of stories are fascinating, many of them are really quite sad.

Women who got married really young and don't know who they are or who are leaving behind difficult situations.

I always say to them: congratulations! Life starts again, and that is so exciting.

For some mothers, the switch from married/cohabiting to single does bring more radical changes, especially where the change in finances is so drastic that it requires a huge shift in lifestyle.

Claire gave up her job in advertising in London to be a full-time wife and mum when she married Mark and the couple had their three children:

He was a high-earning City boy; we didn't need me to work. We moved to the country into this idyllic farmhouse with chickens and pigs and all this land; I kept pinching myself when I looked out of the window, thinking this was my life. And then one day it wasn't. Mark had a breakdown and I realised he had drug and alcohol addictions and enormous debts. He lost his job and I had to take control of the finances and sell the house in a matter of weeks so I could pay off some of his debts, some of which were quite scary. His name was mud in the city so he moved to Russia and I was left with the children, no home and no job. We house-sat for friends and spent the first year living out of our suitcases. Mark sent money occasionally but had very quickly met a new girlfriend in Russia, and I never knew when money was going to appear or not. My mum said to me, 'Darling, you'll just have to be completely independent and if you get any money from Mark, see it as a bonus'.

So that's what I did. First of all I took on some work as a PA for an architect, who I still work for 12 years later, but it's always been part time and I needed an extra income. A friend recommended me to an elderly lady who was looking for help at home and I thought I would give it a go. We got along like a house on fire and when her husband began to develop dementia, she asked if I would help care for him as well. It has been such an incredible experience to work with them both; I have taken a number of dementia care and end-of-life care courses and now look after a couple of other dementia sufferers. I love the work and I know it's something I'll do for the rest of my life.

Sometimes I wonder how I have ended up doing this; it certainly wasn't what I thought I would be doing. I think I'm intrinsically a bit lazy and supporting us all by myself has meant I just can't afford to be lazy! Now I just feel really proud of myself. Two of the children have left home and my youngest is 16. Sometimes wealthier friends don't understand why I can't go on holiday with them or don't just drop everything and go skiing, because they have other people to rely on and do things for them. Social media isn't helpful; sometimes I get a bit down and deflated. But mostly I'm just completely buzzed that I am doing this on my own. It's incredibly empowering.

For solo mums by choice, the change in lifestyle is completely different. They lose the freedoms of their single life rather than gaining them. But it's not always an unwelcome change.

Jas, a musician, found she was pregnant after a one-night-stand and decided to go ahead with the pregnancy by herself. She said:

I used to go out a lot pre-pregnancy. I'm a singer, so being out at gigs was what I did. I was 35 when I found out I was pregnant, so I was lucky in that a lot of my female friends had already had children; I was able to fall very easily into a ready-made mum circuit.

I thought I would miss the gigs and being out and about but I think I was really ready to become a mum, and I just never felt I was missing out on anything. I didn't drink for about four years after Max was born. I just knew I couldn't do anything with even the hint of a hangover so I just cut it out. If I did socialise it was always with other mums at someone's house. Life got a lot smaller, I guess.

As a single person I was already very used to not being invited to things. It's funny how, even now, some of my best friends don't invite me to dinner parties because I'm on my own. It's really shit when you think about it. Do they think I am going to steal their husbands? I don't get it; why don't they just invite another single person to make up the numbers?

But it has made me cultivate a really good tribe of single friends. Single mums, and the women who are in unhappy relationships! I'm fine with it, I choose my friends because I like them, not because their husband might get on with mine or whatever. It's a different life to my coupled-up friends but it's mine and we make it work.

*

After a particularly difficult romantic experience a few years down the line from the split, I gave myself the luxury of some more counselling. I was in quite the mess and feeling hopeless about it all. In one session I expressed my fear that I was never going to meet anyone I wanted to be with, in a full-time sense, again. I felt I was too broken to make anything work, and all the good men were taken.

My counsellor's response really helped because I had never thought about it that way before. Instead of telling me that there are plenty of fish in the sea, or that I just hadn't met the right man yet – promising me a happy ending – she said that women do mostly end up single, when you think about it.

In the UK, average male life expectancy is 79, compared to 82 for women. So there are more of us left standing for one thing. But even if they are alive, then men in their dotage are more likely to marry or remarry younger women. In 2020, there were approximately 2.44 million women aged 65 and over living alone in the UK, compared with 1.26 million men (almost half the women) in the same age group. The rest of them had shacked up with a newer model. So the myth of growing old happily with a husband by your side is in many ways just that, a myth.

She also asked me to think of all the marriages I knew and ask myself if they were truly happy or had been untouched by difficulties and disasters. With a few notable exceptions – my sisters and the friends who had had the good fortune to marry people they still liked – almost every marriage I knew was going through or at least had been through rocky patches: affairs, counselling, splits and reconciliations.

Clearly she didn't mean that men were – are – not worth the effort, as they all leave the party early anyway. Or that marriages couldn't be happy for plenty of people. But it did help me see my future in a different light.

I am still hopelessly devoted to the cause, when it comes to men, despite many attempts to convince myself that I would be far happier as a lesbian. Being proud to be a single mother does not automatically mean I hate men, or would not welcome a nice one into my life, if he came knocking. But her point changed the way I thought about my life then and now. I went from being a failure, who had messed up her chance of being a truly happy married woman, to someone already extremely rich in what I really needed for a happy adult life: my friends.

As the dinner parties of old vanished, new friends had come into my life. Perhaps inevitably I have found myself drawn to other single mums or the women I think of as single-curious: women who are married/cohabiting but have one foot out of their relationships. They haven't jumped yet, and possibly never will, but they come as individuals and live quite separate lives from their partners.

The actress and single mum Pamela Adlon, who writes and stars in the hit show *Better Things*, has a saying that she uses on and off screen: 'all moms are single moms, whether they are married or not.'

I know what she means. Perhaps not all, but definitely some.

There is a kind of nostalgia to these friendships, something of the sixth form about them. As though we have all bunked off school. And in fact we are all the kind of girls who would have been in trouble at school – standing shoulder to shoulder in the headmistress's office. They get into scrapes, these girls. One friend had me howling with laughter when she told how, after a particularly boozy date, she had fallen asleep in the lift in her block of flats and spent a long time going up and down in it – she couldn't be sure how long exactly, but it was enough for her chips to get cold.

Without husbands or significant others to make room for, these friendships seem to grow from a different soil to the girls' nights and weekends of my married friendships. Free from any unspoken rules about competition and wifeliness, they feel somehow more organic but also more supportive: women without other 'halves' who bring their whole selves and are teaming up to face whatever comes their way, together. My friends have become like aunties; my children look forward to visits from these dazzling and often raucous women who fill the house with cackles and dance in the kitchen. They sidle onto the sofa sometimes or lie down on the grass if we are in the garden and listen to us talking, quietly taking everything in.

They are not intrinsically better or more significant than the friendships enjoyed by married/cohabiting people. But they are, I think, more authentically functional, more interdependent than the friendships I experienced as a married woman, more steeped in solidarity and understanding. When, during an especially busy time with work, my best friend turned up at my door unannounced and took my dog out for a walk, I felt tears of gratitude well up in my eyes as I watched them bumble off down the road. I rely on my friends, and they on me, more because we have to, and in that reliance comes a deeper connection and understanding. A friend in need is, after all, a friend indeed.

In his book *Happy Ever After*, Professor Paul Dolan shows with statistics and research that it is in fact single people who report greater happiness and enjoy larger social networks than married couples. He doesn't so much deconstruct as completely annihilate the many narrative constructs we in Western society live and die by in the name of so-called happiness. He says:

> ...single people are more likely to foster connections that bring them fulfilment, whereas married people often find themselves with less consciously chosen social networks, such as a spouse's family members... married and cohabiting individuals tend to become more socially isolated... This is not to say that wider social networks are always good for us, just that there might be some important upsides to being single that the marriage narrative ignores.[34]

There is so much to be said for the friendships you make in single motherhood that are not determined by your marital status or your spouse's compatibility with your friend's husband, or your children being similar ages or the fact that you wait in the same school playground every day. Friendships that are instead about you, your personality, the things that interest you, the people you are drawn to and whose company you enjoy, just because.

And yet beyond the occasional buddy movie, there is little recognition of female friendship in our culture, no way to celebrate these unions. As soon as we turn 21, all our ceremonies and rites of passage

34 Paul Dolan (2020) *Happy Ever After: A Radical New Approach to Living Well*. London: Penguin, page 78.

are about romantic love: engagement, marriage, anniversaries. We invite all our friends to these celebrations to toast us and share the joy, and yet we don't give similar dues to the very relationships that fill the room with laughter and love: our friendships.

Splendid isolation

Those early weekends all alone with nowhere to go when the children were with their dad had been a shock to my system, but as time went on, we all grew into different versions of ourselves and the things that mattered at the start didn't seem to matter so much any more. For one thing, the children got older – as they tend to – and became more concerned with seeing their friends, or else their technology. Their toys shrank in volume from full shelves full of boxes full of things full of stuff, to one single screen and a pair of headphones each. As the toys vanished I became less someone to play with and more someone to facilitate their play dates and buy their PlayStation vouchers. Where once I had to force myself to watch *In the Night Garden* with them, I increasingly found myself hoping they'd want to stop by the lounge and watch something with me. (Thank you, Netflix, for *Stranger Things*. On reflection I still believe the nightmares were worth it.) They started to make their own lunches and think for themselves about what they were going to wear or which friends they were going to see at the weekend.

I got older too. And as Stevie Nicks sang, time makes you bolder. The time alone was no longer something to be endured with drawer organising or blotted out with boozy nights – although both of those things can still happen. But I began to cherish the empty house, when I could potter around and make phone calls and water plants and talk to myself and titivate with the way things were arranged on a shelf, without any interruptions. Or the freedom of walking breezily out of the door on a Saturday morning to meet a friend, with only a small bag over my shoulder and no one to give a lift to at all, all day. I liked not planning dinner or buying (yes, it's true) a ready meal for myself, which I would eat shamelessly in front of the television in jogging bottoms and no bra, the cat on one side and the dog on the other. If I had a boyfriend, I liked feeling like a whole person who could enjoy an adult connection, not someone whose mind was always slightly elsewhere, hiding from the children or worrying about what time they'd be back. I liked having room in my head to think and to have ideas.

Of course spending time alone isn't the exclusive member benefit of single mothers who are co-parenting, but knowing it was coming, regularly, seemed like a too-generous benefits package in a new job. I couldn't quite believe it was okay at times. That guilt again. We have long normalised the need for men to retreat to their sheds and man caves in order to be alone, yet the idea that a woman might need or enjoy the luxury of her own space – not to work or to spend it away with friends or visiting places, but just because? That seemed, still does seem, almost preposterous.

In the history of all humankind, men have been recognised as the great artists and inventors, designers and builders. (Of course, there is an issue with the writing of history and the fact that men tended not to include women in their history books – E.H. Gombrich's *The Story of Art*, the first textbook on my History of Art degree all those years ago, is the most famous example of a 'definitive' history that entirely excluded and ignored women artists.[35]) But even taking that into account, the overwhelming majority of creative 'progress' has been achieved by men.

Caitlin Moran writes, in *How to Be a Woman*:

Let's stop exhaustingly pretending that there is a parallel history of women being victorious and creative, on an equal with men, that's just been comprehensively covered up by

---

35 E.H. Gombrich (1950/2007) *The Story of Art*. London: Phaidon Press.

The Man. There isn't. Our empires, armies, cities, artworks, philosophers, philanthropists, inventors, scientists, astronauts, explorers, politicians and icons could all fit, comfortably, into one of the private karaoke booths in Singstar. We have no Mozart; no Einstein; no Galileo; no Gandhi. No Beatles, no Churchill, no Hawking, no Columbus. It just didn't happen. Nearly everything so far has been the creation of men.[36]

And what did all these men have in common? Was it their superior brainpower? Or was it simply that they had the time? Men have always had time on their hands to do what they liked with, studios and rooms to retreat to, and wives servicing their needs. They don't call it splendid isolation for nothing.

Good news klaxon: single mothers get time! Not all of us, but lots of us if we are lucky enough to have another parent who isn't a dirtbag. We get time when our children are being looked after by someone who really cares about them, and I think this fact is quietly kind of radical. Whether it is one night a week or every other weekend or half of the week or once a month, we do get time off to do what we please. To read, to work, to have mindless fun, to rest, to cry or stare into space. The point is not what we do with it but that it is ours.

In this sense, I can't help coming back to the thought that being a single mother is a major act of self-care. A way of putting in boundaries and creating space – physical and emotional – for yourself, in a way that our married/cohabiting sisters cannot always do so regularly and in such distinct chunks of time. A way of retaining a tiny smidge of yourself when the rest of it is has been devoured by everyone else.

No one had heard of self-care when we split up, but these days self-care – the idea that you look after yourself in whatever way you feel is necessary to protect and nourish your physical and mental

---

36 Caitlin Moran (2011) *How to Be a Woman*. London: Ebury Press.

wellbeing – it's everywhere. We are all switched on to the idea that you cannot pour from an empty cup. Whether it's yoga and bubble baths or roller-derby and journaling, the idea that in a world gone mad, we need to take more care of ourselves, has gained enough traction to now be normal.

I'd be lying if I said that I spend all of my child- and work-free time having Reiki and doing Nordic walking. The truth is that much of it is spent on catch-up tasks: cleaning the house, working, sleeping. If these sound like unimaginative ways to fill the time, that is because they are. I do not recommend any of these pastimes to other new single mothers who find themselves with a whole weekend free of children. And yet if that is the way you want to spend it, then that's fine too, isn't it? Sometimes hard work is its own reward. Whatever gets you through.

I would also be lying if I said I always relish the time my children are with their father. I am not always deliriously happy to be without them and I am no stranger to the green-eyed monster. The deep, animal sense that the children are mine and belong by my side at all times still occasionally wells up in me, Gollum-like. Not knowing what they are having for tea, not knowing who is at their other house, not knowing what is being said or overheard, and not really being entitled to know either: relinquishing the lead, even if it is only for a weekend, can be teeth-grindingly hard.

When they were younger, it was mostly in the physical sense of missing them, finding it strange not to be able to hear them in the next room. Now they are older, they are rarely not in touch by text, asking what's for tea later or for something they have left here to be located. Daughters especially seem to need to keep you informed of all their movements, and I am always happy that she wants to send me a picture of her latest drawing or of her with the dog from her dad's house. The worry now they are older and moodier – their world full of social media and porn, vaping and self-harming, and all the other terrifying headlines that accompany teens – is more that they might be unhappy or in a situation where they need me, and I wouldn't necessarily know.

Again I have to remind myself that plenty of children in dual-parent households keep secrets and lead lives their parents don't know about. And in having two sets of parents and two households, they actually have more opportunities to talk to whichever adult they need to. Their horizons are broader, they have options. I have also learned that to try to stay involved while they are with their father or to try to interrogate them when they come home is a fruitless task that no one enjoys or benefits from. For one thing, they make terrible reporters. But also, asking too many questions seems only to dig a greater divide for all of us. In the end, there is no way around it: missing your children is something single mothers who are co-parenting simply have to go through. While it's not particularly enjoyable, it is usually short term, and, like a general anaesthetic, it is very often over before you know it has begun.

The American writer and feminist Audre Lorde wrote in *A Burst of Light*: 'Caring for myself is not self-indulgence. It is self-preservation, and that is an act of political warfare.'[37]

Warfare might be taking it a bit far when all you're doing is heating up a Waitrose lasagne and watching *Magic Mike*. But there is a sense of resistance, something undeniably powerful, about this aspect of the single motherhood experience. Does it scare people, I wonder, what we might do with all this power if we are allowed to run free with it? Is that why we still seem to stamp on single mothers and who they are and everything they stand for? In case we tell the others about what happens when we are not tending the children or marinading the chicken breasts?

Not all single mothers are lucky enough to be able to co-parent with someone who loves their child as much as they do, who they

---

37 Audre Lorde (2017) *A Burst of Light: And Other Essays* (first published 1988). Long Island, NY: Ixia Press.

can trust and who doesn't charge them. In particular single mothers by choice don't get the luxury of another parent to take the strain. But being single mothers by choice, and therefore the kind of women who know exactly what they need and how to get it, they seem to have it covered.

Rowan says:

> I have very reliable babysitters and I get a sitter at least once a week. And my dad takes Kit on Sunday mornings so I can run with a friend. I know other single mums by choice who have a group and swap sleepovers. I think it's essential to my sanity to have some time alone. I'm quite good at looking after myself on that front. I'm not sure everyone is.

Lara makes a special effort to treat herself and make sure she gets the gift she really wants – time to herself: 'Last Saturday the boys were with the nanny, and I bought myself some expensive flowers and went to St Michael's Lane hotel and had a glass of champagne at eleven o'clock in the morning by myself. It was amazing. I'll be doing the same again soon.'

And single mothers who are doing it by themselves, perhaps because the father has gone AWOL, are equally as resourceful when it comes to getting a break.

'My neighbour and I take it in turns to have each other's kids every weekend,' says Natalie. 'It means we get a whole weekend to ourselves, but the kids don't feel like they are away from home too much. It's actually perfect – I get a whole weekend off every fortnight!'

We don't talk enough about this – the freedom we get and what it makes possible. When you announce your separation no one says: 'OMG lucky you! You'll get every other weekend off and can finally write that book/set up that business/cure the common cold!' Instead people tell us how sorry they are, as if the only thing that we have ever wanted is to be at home washing things.

As Paul Dolan reflects in *Happily Ever After*: 'We should perhaps start using the word "congratulations" for divorce, as well as marriage.'[38]

Welcome to the village

Not long after we split, I became preoccupied with thoughts about what would happen to the children if I died. I blame my solicitor, who, as soon as we began divorce proceedings, recommended I rewrote my will so that all my many millions would not automatically be left to my ex-husband and would instead go directly to my children (to be looked after by my sisters until they were old enough to get their mitts on it). This was sound advice, and I was naturally delighted to be able to spend a bit more money on my legal fees, but it got me thinking: what would happen to them if I died? Of course, they would go and live with their dad and he would look after them well, and my sisters and all my family would all still be in their lives. They would not be separated or sent to live with cruel aunts like James in *James and the Giant Peach*, or unscrupulous guardians like the children in Lemony Snicket's *A Series of Unfortunate Events* (children's literature does seem to feature a disproportionate number of stories about orphaned children being sent to live with horrible people).

But, selfishly, I couldn't stop thinking about how I would stay in their lives. Their dad and I were such opposites we ran on entirely different operating systems, a living error message that seemed only to get louder the longer we spent apart. Who would make sure they got the advice that I would give them or buy them the Christmas and birthday presents that I would choose? How would they know what I would say or hear the stories I hadn't told them yet, about all the places I had lived, or my first job or learning to drive? How

---

38 Paul Dolan (2020) *Happy Ever After: A Radical New Approach to Living Well*. London: Penguin.

would I still be there, even though I wasn't? I'd read about women who knew they were dying and left letters for their children to open every year on their birthdays. Every time I tried to even think about writing them a letter, I cried too much to start it.

Feeling that I needed to do something about this, I asked two of my best male friends and two of my best girlfriends if they would take on the responsibility of being my agents. I wanted the children to know that when it came to major life stuff, like choosing what to study at university or deciding what direction to take with their careers, they could get in touch with this panel of trusted advisors and get the kind of feedback they might get from me. Of course they all said yes, and I cried a bit more. It's something I hope will never need to happen, and they've probably forgotten about it now anyway. They're probably reading this now, wondering if it was them I asked (Debs, Lisa, Nick and Richard, it's you). But it was a relief to know I had put it out there. As much of a relief as writing that will had been, anyway.

You have to get good at asking for help when you are a single mother. The old African proverb that it takes a village to raise a child is true for all of us, no matter what our circumstances. The teachers and the childminders, the sports coaches and the grandparents and the friends – we are all surrounded by villagers who help us raise our children.

But as a single mother you sometimes have to work a bit harder to be a part of the same village as everyone else. Villages, like dinner parties, tend to be built on foundations dug in with gender-archetypes, even in the twenty-first century: the dads play golf or go cycling together, the mums have weekends away and meet for coffees. It's harder to be a relevant, purposeful member of the village sometimes when there is only one of you.

Fiona describes how as a solo mum in her local Jewish community, she found herself being ostracised, not deliberately, but in a kind of benign way:

My son went to a really small school; it was a new Jewish school so his form was the first form and the first year. It was really tiny. As a result all the parents were very involved. Often the mums would take the girls on trips and the dads would take the boys, so my son would not be invited because he didn't have a dad to bring him along, and it wouldn't have been appropriate for me to go along with them or for us to join the girls. Or the men would have whisky nights and of course I wasn't invited to those either. It was really difficult and upsetting at the time.

Psychologist Joanne Fortune says it's always important to look after the person who is doing the looking after, whatever the situation, and that single mothers might need to work a bit harder at making that happen: 'Single mums who don't have a partner need to identify their "others", the people who will be there for them and their children.' She adds:

No one is ever really parenting alone – we have grandparents, uncles, aunts. Even without family there are health visitors and support groups and people who are there to help and give that wrap-around support. The main thing is that you identify your safety network. Get good at asking for help – people won't say yes if they don't want to.

It could be as simple as saying to a friend that it would be really helpful if your child could go there after school one day every week until you finish your work or asking another parent to give your child a lift to swimming club, says Fortune.

Ruth, a solo mum by choice, asked a friend's husband if she could pay him to take her son out for a couple of hours every week. She said:

Raffy is only two but I can see how much he enjoys male company; his eyes light up whenever we meet a man. There aren't really any men in my life, so I asked Jim (my friend's husband) if I could pay him or one of his teenage sons to take him to the park and do some activities with him. Jim refused to let me pay him and what I thought was really sweet was that both of his teenage sons offered to help as well. They won't take a penny for it. I think they all really enjoy the chance to play!

I know I have corralled my brother-in-law into playing table tennis with my son and gladly accepted my sister's offers of shopping drops and pharmacy runs when I have been unwell. I've relied on lifts to and from activities from other parents. I've dispatched my children to stay with friends in the holidays, called on a friend's husband to pick me up when my car broke down, and I have gladly accepted every single offer of a sleepover that has ever been made. I know I've also subjected my sisters and many of my friends to the kind of parenting discussions that I might normally have had with a husband or partner: should they move school, should I be worried about this, what do you think this behaviour is about? In an ideal world their dad and I would talk these things through, but it's not always possible. Without the good counsel of my friends and my family, I'm not sure I would ever make any decisions. Not the right ones, anyway.

Grandma, we love you

But the person who has really been my safety network and my significant other has been my own mum. We all know how important grandparents are by now. Not only are they full of great stories and are fully prepared to listen, with genuine interest, to your child talking about *Octonauts* for three hours straight, but they are often retired and reasonably agile, making them incredibly well qualified for the job of childminder.

According to an ICM poll in 2020, over a third of grandparents now spend three or more days a week looking after their grandchildren as unpaid childcare. Women are going back to work earlier because of the finances, and grandparents are stepping in to hold the babies. Of course what we really mean when we say grandparents is grandmothers. Grandads might be in the same house, sure, but it's the grandmothers who are really baking the gingerbread men and having the tea parties, picking them up from pre-school and wiping all the bottoms. I remember when my dad was alive and the children were small his thing was to sit in his armchair and throw cushions at them as they ran past him – they loved this game, it's true, but it also very cleverly ensured he didn't have to get out of his chair.

I relied heavily on my mum when the children were small; she had them both for two days a week so I could return to work. They were older by the time the divorce came around, but her house was and still is their second home, where they feel they can fling themselves on the sofa after school and open the biscuit tin without asking. We get to her house and they both disappear: my daughter to the bedroom where she sits at Mum's dressing table (because only grandmas have dressing tables), trying on jewellery and silk scarves, while my son sequesters himself, phone in hand, into the sheepskins and blankets on her big cosy sofa while we discuss the matters of the day. She is the first person we call when there is exciting news, the person who makes all three of us feel loved.

Unsurprisingly, grandmothers play a huge part in the support network of single mums (And some research suggests that the single mum and single grandmother model is a 'growth' lifestyle choice. In 2010, the British Social Attitudes survey showed that more than half – 53 per cent – of grandmothers who do not have a husband or male partner are likely to have daughters who are also single mothers. This figure is up from 44 per cent two years earlier.)

Practically every single mum I know has a mum of their own, whether they are single, widowed or still married to Grandad, who has stepped in to help in a major way. Ruth says:

> Mum comes every Wednesday and basically gives me the day off. And if I want to go out she stays over. And she always does my ironing and changes my sheets – it's like having a fairy godmother come to stay every week. No matter how stressful the week is just knowing that I have that day coming is enough to get me through.

And while most of us will know instinctively how the presence of a grandparent in any child's life can bring many benefits, from boosting language skills to being the world's most reliable source of sweets, the helpful scientists at Oxford University have done some research to make the importance of the maternal grandmother to the single mother and her children official.

Dr Sarah Harper at the University of Oxford's Institute of Ageing looked more closely at the role grandmothers play in single mother families and how they can become both replacement partners and parents (the report uses the title 'lone mother' which I find annoying but will have to forgive). The report concludes:

> Maternal grandmothers in general are found to be important stress reducers, either through emotional support or through practical intervention and support, to their lone mother daughters. The roles of replacement parent and partner seem to be of significant importance for the lone mothers as the motivation for this arrangement seems to be twofold. On one hand, these changing roles derive from the subjective experience of missing

structures in their own lives (being a single parent and being without a partner) and, on the other, from the feelings they experience due to the missing structures in their children's lives.

When asked how they view their mothers' grandparenting, most interviewees state they view it as a role of being both a mother to them and a grandmother to their grandchildren and that both of these relationship connections are giving equal motivation for their grandparenting behavior. It seems important for mothers to feel that grandparenting is more than simply a new form of parenting and parental support. It is a relationship with equal importance and significance for all of the family members; it is a network for mutual support, which increases the wellbeing of all involved.

Basically, the great thing about a grandmother is that she is as invested in the mother as in the child – harking back to Joanna Fortune's point about looking after the looker-after. And, says Harper, the relationship works for Grandma, too, as it is a salve for the common losses experienced by older women as husbands and friends pass away.

Taking the grandma principle even further, in her book *Mom Genes*, Abigail Tucker looks at the science behind the mother-child bond and reveals, among other things, how maternal grandmothers are actually more important for the survival of an infant than their biological fathers. She says:

As welcome as human paternal presence and activity may be, as indebted as we may feel for our mates' grilled-cheese slinging and stroller patrols, that's all gravy in the evolutionist's cold-eyed view, where what matters at the end of the day is who dies and who survives. For humans across cultures, according to scientists who've run the numbers, the presence of a nearby grandma seems to be more of a boon to child's survival than a dad is. Some go further, contending that dads are essentially irrelevant to child survival.[39]

Or to put it another way: in a game of survival rock, paper, scissors, maternal grandmothers beat dads. Maybe this is something single mums have always known.

Let's all live in a mommune

One of the recurring jokes of the early years of motherhood, when I was having coffee with friends and we were all complaining about our husbands and how unhelpful they were, was that we should all live in a commune. We'd help each other out and the kids would always have friends to play with and life would generally be much better and nicer. That was the joke.

For a growing number of single mums, this kind of mutual living arrangement with friends in the same boat is becoming a reality. With the cost of housing pricing single women with children out of the market, they are clubbing together to live in 'mommunes'.

It's a more established lifestyle choice in the US where there are over 15 million single mothers, with over 30 per cent of them living in poverty (compared to around 8 per cent of married couple families). Property services like CoAbode and RoomMatesWithKids have sprung up, founded by single parents seeking a different approach, and are specifically geared towards single parents who are looking to share their home and all the associated demands and costs of single parenting, with others.

It's happening in the UK too, as single mums outsmart the dual-income mortgage model and pool their resources to buy homes big enough for two or three single-mother families.

---

39 Abigail Tucker (2021) *Mom Genes: Inside the New Science of Our Ancient Maternal Instinct.* New York: Simon & Schuster.

One single mum, Janet Hoggarth, even wrote a series of books based on the life she and her children shared in the 'single mums' mansion':

> I'd been a single mum for about 18 months and if I'm honest was struggling with it all. I was really questioning who I was and what my place in the world was. When my friend Vicky's partner left her only a few months after their baby had been born, I suggested she move in with me and my two (I had a two-year-old and a five-year-old at that stage). It was only supposed to be for a few months while she got back on her feet, but it ended up being two years! Around the same time I bumped into another friend who I hadn't seen for ages – we hardly recognised each other because we'd both lost so much weight. It turned out she had also recently become a single mum and lived up the road from us, so she became part of our commune too.
>
> We all appreciated having another adult around to laugh, and cry, with. There was so much going on for all of us with divorces and separations, we all leant on each other. It made all of us feel more secure, I think.
>
> It also made the house feel more like a home. The children all loved having each other around. It had been such a difficult time at first but when the others moved in the atmosphere changed. We had lots of parties. We had all three of us been sociable people and found that the dinner party invitations stopped coming when we were no longer married, so we had our own parties instead.
>
> Apparently we inspired a number of other mommunes: friends of friends who heard what we'd done and set up with others in the same boat. I know one group of mums who have lived together for ten years now. I look back on that time and have some of the best and fondest memories.

Finding your tribe

One of the great things about social media is the way it allows people to find new tribes in different places. Geography and proximity don't necessarily need to dictate your tribal allegiance any more. No surprise then that single parents are creating their own virtual tribes and in the UK it's all about one platform: Frolo. The Frolo Community app (Frolo stands for Friends/Solo) makes it easy for single parents to connect with likeminded single parents in the same area as well as a wider online community of single parents for friendship, meet-ups, advice and all-round support.

Frolo was founded by single mum Zoe Desmond, whose relationship with her son's father ended shortly after her son turned one. She says:

> I had lots of friends and family but I didn't know any other single parents at all and felt completely isolated in my experience. And I felt a lot of shame. I remember being in a taxi. I'd been away for the weekend with my son, and the taxi driver asked where my husband was. I told him I didn't have one and he said, 'What do you mean?' and as I said, 'I'm a single mum' I almost burst into tears. I could hardly even say it.
>
> I found myself wishing the weekends away, as all I could see were families everywhere and the weekends seemed to go on forever. All these feelings: loneliness, overwhelm and guilt for not being the mum I wanted to be for Billy. The only thing that gave me hope was thinking about connecting with other people in my situation. I began to imagine being able to go on playdates, have Sunday lunches and weekend adventures with other single parents like me. I felt frustrated because I knew that 1 in 4 families are single parent families but had no way of connecting with any who were local to me with kids the same age!

I went online and looked at the various mum apps and websites, but nothing seemed to be working specifically for single parents. Pages on Facebook all felt quite negative and not in line with what I wanted life to be like. I started imagining what my perfect solution would be. I was never looking for a business idea, I just wished it existed. The Frolo Community took off immediately – as it turns out, I was not the only one wishing for an easy way to connect with other single parents. The app now has over 30,000 users and Frolo Dating – the world's first user-verified single-parent dating app –launches in 2022.

Frolo has completely changed my world and my son's world. All of the things I was missing back then – the single parent friends, the connection, the support – I have it all now, in abundance. Seeing other frolos forge friendships and really embrace and feel empowered by their single parent lives is something that makes me feel incredibly proud.

Shine bright

It's the systems that are in place, the traditions and the stereotypes, that make everyday life more challenging for the single mother. The family deals and two-for-one tickets, the double occupancy, the lads'n'dads sports, the dinner parties for eight. We are trying to function on an ancient, groaning power network that still burns traditional family fossil fuels.

But if you can find a way to circumvent the system – and if you are a single mother then I'm willing to bet that you're already the kind of person who is pretty good at circumventing things, either by nature or through hard-earned experience – then it is entirely possible to live a bright and brilliant life plugged into a different kind of grid.

Far from being lonely, lone, solo, single or sad, you may find that your world gets bigger and your heart fuller as you make more connections with people and places that you like and choose for yourself. You have stronger and more meaningful friendships, your relationship with family can become even more precious, and you gain a greater sense of yourself and what you are truly capable of. You find out who you really are.

Some tips for living your best single mum life

Try to do something for yourself in the time that the children are away with their other parent (if they have one). Even if it is only something small like meeting a friend for coffee or taking a class at the leisure centre, these are the first building blocks of a new life that you get to design for yourself. Making the time away from them meaningful to you is the best way to stay positive.

If you are struggling to adjust to the time away from your children, I find doing something small for them, like making a cake or sprucing up their room, can help me feel like I'm still being their mum, even if they're not at home.

Rest. Being a single parent can be relentless, physically and emotionally. Grasp with both hands any opportunities for a nap or just some peace and quiet whenever they arise. You have to save your strength and be your own carer for now – look after yourself the way you would a friend or a partner.

Leave toxic friendships. Now is a very good time to take a mental audit of the people in your life. Friendships can expire in the way that relationships do and there is no room now for spreading yourself too thin in life. If someone is no longer making a positive contribution or they're just generally making you a bit miserable, then setting yourself free can be an extremely positive step. Life is too short for people who aren't rooting for you.

Get on top of your finances, even if it means facing some difficult truths. The stress of financial worry is not good for you. Prioritise your financial stability and get help with this if you need it. No one teaches you how to manage your household finances so it's OK to admit that you don't know where to start. There are plenty of resources out there, like MoneySavingExpert.com. There are also some great female financial influencers on social media, giving you tips on how to manage your money. I love Gemma Bird, aka Money Mum, for her real and practical advice like having a 'no-spend day' and ditching the Starbucks when you are out and about.

Accept and ask for help. Independence can be strangely intoxicating at times; there is something alluring about being able to do it all by yourself. But no single mum is an island and learning to accept help when it is offered to you will serve you and your children far better in the long run. Good people like to help others. Surround yourself with good people, because you are a good person too.

Set up a WhatsApp group with other single mums so you can pool resources and share costs. It could be something small like borrowing luggage for a trip to something more regular like childcare swaps and babysitting.

And a few more ideas from Zoe Desmond at Frolo

Connect with other single parents in your area! It makes such an incredible difference to how supported you feel. Obviously you can do this via Frolo, where we have regular real-life meet-ups and virtual nights out that happen every Friday. People are often a bit sceptical at first but once they take the plunge and get involved they never look back.

Make plans so you have things to look forward to. There are certain times, like the summer holidays, Christmas, Sundays, when it can be easy to feel isolated. Having fun stuff to look forward to makes life feel so much easier.

Embrace and encourage your children's friendships with other children from single parent families. The more we can normalise the experience the happier everyone will be, and being happy helps you be the best parent you can be.

Be proud of yourself! Parenting is hard, single parenting is even harder and definitely not for the faint-hearted. Take a minute to be kind to yourself, and have some self-love and admiration for all that you are achieving.

CHAPTER SIX

Where Is My Happy Ending?

Fear not, she hath risen!
Moira Rose, *Schitt's Creek*

As I write this, it is almost exactly eight years since my children's dad and I split up. The divorce has only just been finalised. People are always amazed when I tell them how long it has taken and imagine we have been locked in a vicious court battle over all of our properties, offshore investments and custody of the children.

But the truth is it took so long because it is so expensive, time-consuming and extremely boring indeed. We didn't have much to divide up and we agreed the childcare arrangements between ourselves. Even so, we had to keep stopping for a break in the proceedings because one or both of us couldn't afford the next round of solicitors' fees, or simply didn't have the emotional or mental reserves for the next bout of pointless paperwork and overly complicated language.

It's hardly news that the British divorce system is archaic, even with supposed 'quickies' which, as far as I can tell, are like the fabled £1 flights to Ibiza – they sound great but somehow never materialise and seem to always come with a whole load of hidden extras no one told you you had to buy. But still, it's hard not to be outraged by the whole ugly process, which, like Child Maintenance, appears to have been drawn up by someone using a quill, with the aim not of helping anyone actually dissolve their marriage efficiently and painlessly, but to make doing so difficult and shameful, a process to be avoided at all costs, literally and figuratively. A process designed to keep people – by which of course I mostly mean women – married. Because it is women who want to get divorced more than men. In the US, four out of five divorces are filed by women. Paul Dolan writes: 'The narrative may nudge them into marriage but, once there, they eventually realise the raw deal they are getting and want to get out'.[40] The same does not hold for cohabiting couples, says Dolan, where men and women tend to end relationships equally. 'There is something special about the historically subordinating institution of marriage that women want to escape from more than men.'[41]

I can't imagine the marriage craze coming to an end any time soon, but does divorce really still have to be like this? Wouldn't it be so much nicer for everyone if all that time and money, all those clever solicitors and judges with all that education and all those gavels, spent their time helping parents navigate their divorces with their children in mind, giving them advice on how to make the whole thing go smoothly and how best to manage their money and how to stay friends, instead of pitting couples against each other and advising us all how to bleed each other dry.

'We always say if people knew how much it costs to get divorced, they'd never get married!' joked my solicitor's secretary recently, as I handed over another large sum of money I could have really done with. I didn't laugh.

Anyway, it's done now. And although I have not considered myself to be married for the past eight years, I've been surprised by how it finally being over is a load off that I didn't realise I was

40 Paul Dolan (2020) *Happy Ever After: A Radical New Approach to Living Well*. London: Penguin, page 74.

41 Paul Dolan (2020) *Happy Ever After: A Radical New Approach to Living Well*. London: Penguin.

carrying. There is, as Dolan says, something in the narrative that lures you in. The flipside of this lure means when the narrative comes to a close, you feel like you've just escaped from a high-security prison where you were being held for a crime you didn't commit.

It would have been easy in some ways to simply stay married and avoid the costs and the administrative headache of it all. I've certainly met quite a few people who have chosen this route. If it's only a piece of paper, why should it matter whether you are divorced or not? There are plenty of reasons, mostly mortgage and credit related, why it is helpful to not be married to someone you're not living with. But I would also recommend it on an emotional level for both parties in the arrangement. There is something in the file being closed that makes everything following on seem lighter and less fraught. Like handing in an essay you have really struggled to finish. Or returning something you borrowed. A clean slate. Relief.

Putting that final seal on the deal also inspires retrospection of course. Looking back over the past eight years I see how so much about single motherhood has changed, in the wider world, but also in my mind's eye.

There has been a cultural shift, for sure. Single mothers – successful, happy, funny ones – are on our screens and in our bookshops more and more. In Netflix's *Sex Education*, one of its most successful shows ever, the main character is an empowered single mum (played by real-life empowered single mum, Gillian Anderson) and sex therapist, whose one-night stands are regular guests at the breakfast table with her teenage son, Otis. It's hard to imagine that show happening, even just eight years ago. *Maid*, the story of a single mother escaping domestic abuse, was a *New York Times* bestseller and Netflix hit. *Mare of Easttown*, about a grumpy middle-aged single mum (and grandma) detective and *Better Things*, a show about a single mother and actress raising three daughters in LA, have both won critical acclaim. And Katherine Ryan's comedy

The Duchess portrayed a happily single, wealthy woman on the hunt for a sperm donor to give her daughter a sibling.

It can only be a good thing, not only for single mothers and their children, but for pretty much everyone else, to see and engage with these multifaceted, surprising and deeply inspiring stories of single mums' lives. If Netflix is now a mirror to the world, then I suspect we'll be seeing plenty more of our stories reflected over the coming years.

I've changed, too, of course. No one needs to hear another middle-aged woman banging on about how liberated she feels and how much she doesn't care what you think of her any more, but I can confirm that this change does come. Whether it's from simple life experience, or all 637 of the self-help books I have read (kind of), or some kind of evolutionary switch going off – or on – you do just start to think: fuck it. This is me. Take me or leave me. I'm not going on another diet.

But more than that, I know that single motherhood constantly asks me to push myself beyond my own boundaries. It can be small things, like having the confidence now to correct people when they call me Mrs (I didn't get divorced so I could be called Mrs for the rest of my life; I prefer Ms, and no one calls me Miss anymore anyway because I'm so old), to bigger stuff, like doing Christmas morning presents as a trio – which turns out to be just as lovely as it ever was, and maybe even lovelier; perhaps because it's not so frantic it can be really savoured (it helps that they no longer get up at four o'clock in the morning). And doing Christmas Day without them – a day off that can be just what the doctor ordered at the end of a busy December. I have come to enjoy the years when it is their dad's turn and he picks them up and we all have a nice festive coffee, and I am then free to go to my sister's house and legitimately drink quite a lot of Champagne before mid-day.

It can also be big stuff, like taking the kids on holiday on my own. I have been surprised by how much I get from travelling with my children, just the three of us. It would be easy to imagine it hard work, relentless and tiring without another adult on hand to help. It can be all of those things, but equally it is an opportunity for us to spend time together when we are not concerned with humdrum matters of laundry and homework. I am more fun to be with at the same time as their curiosity is heightened, whether it is by how to read a departures board at the train station or discovering what the pastries are like in a Spanish supermarket. We have to collaborate and find our way to places together, and we have different conversations and experiences as a result. I'm in a more playful frame of mind, whether that is counting the number of willies on display in an art gallery or swimming races in the hotel pool. All the great things about travel – even if it is only a night away to stay with friends – seem to be magnified, a more shared experience that means more somehow, when it is just me and them. And while travel as a single parent can feel like it costs twice the price just to leave the house, like so much of this game, it is also twice the joy and twice the fun.

Cycling through Amsterdam a few summers ago, watching them wind their way so confidently through the city, was a mental Polaroid moment. Riding a bike wasn't really part of my childhood – I grew up in Birmingham where the bus was king of the road – and I never thought I'd ride one through a major European capital. And yet here I was doing exactly that with my own children. I felt quietly proud of us all on that trip, even if there were loads of cycle lanes. And even though I have no Dutch ancestry or connections to the country at all, and getting the plot and permissions is probably an administrative nightmare, especially post-Brexit; in fact the whole thing is a terrible idea – I've told them I'd be happy to be buried in the city's beautiful cemetery that we cycled through that day. Morbid as it sounds, I felt really happy there.

It depends on how you define happy and what a happy life means to you. But for me, being on this learning curve, gruelling and slippery as it can feel at times, but always moving up and forward, is what makes me feel alive.

Growing older has also meant that more of my contemporaries have split up. Everyone who is anyone is divorced now. We were quite early adopters with our separation, and this might have been why the news of our split seemed to come with all those shock waves at the time. As the years have gone by, other couples in my circle and friends outside it, have called time on their relationships, met new partners, moved to new places. Even Ben Affleck and Jennifer Lopez have split up and gotten back together. My sister, a primary school teacher, remarked recently that in her class a traditional nuclear family is a peculiarity now. Are we approaching peak married? Who knows. But as she said, we've all got to find a way of living alongside our exes and new partners and all the other extras who appear, because it's more normal not to be normal these days.

There's still plenty of work to do. While mums like Melanie Rashford are still going hungry and the newspapers think it's somehow a good news story the fight is not over. Where should we start?

Policy that acknowledges single mothers and their contribution would be nice. Victoria Benson, CEO of Gingerbread, says: 'Single mums were treated so unfairly throughout the Covid-19 pandemic. At the start, when there were no bubbles at all, single parents couldn't even share parenting with the other parent or meet anyone else. It was incredibly hard; any connection or support you had was withdrawn and nobody in government seemed to think about that. Even things like going to the shops, not being able to take their child into a supermarket – we heard from so many single parents who were challenged for having their child with them but they really didn't have a choice. They were just forgotten, I think.

'We've also seen a reduction in flexible working hours. We are back to the same levels as the 1990s. There are very few part-time jobs and single mums need part-time work because of their caring responsibilities. It also often doesn't pay for them to work full time because they so rarely recover the costs of childcare. Childcare is extremely expensive and there is very little availability, so it has become harder, not easier, to be a single mother. It's not very cheery.

'Often it just seems that single parents are overlooked by policymakers. They're just not considered.'

Obviously, systemic change from the top, with policies that acknowledge and compensate for the childcare disparity faced by single mothers, fairer pricing and appropriate tax breaks would all be good ways to start changing things.

But these sorts of major cultural and societal changes aren't going to happen overnight What can we do at a more grassroots level, to shift the perception of single mothers and make life as a single mum less burdened by stigma as well as the practical challenges?

Throughout the writing of this book, I have been struck by the many ways in which solo and single mums by choice get it so right. From the way their single motherhood journey begins (by choice), to the way they discuss their family situation with their children and the way they approach their subsequent adult relationships, there is an intentionality and a balls-out pride to the way they experience single motherhood. As my Instagram feed has become increasingly populated by empowered single mothers, from financial experts to attachment theory therapists, I've seen the phrase 'high-value woman' appear more frequently and this is how I think of single mothers by choice: women who know their worth and aren't afraid to expect the best for themselves. What can we common-or-garden single mums, those of us who have stumbled into this without our glasses on, glean from them? How can we all feel more like high-value women?

Talking and open communication is such a big part of the solo mums' toolkit. The Donor Conception Network's Talking and Telling programme supports parents in telling their children about their origins and differences according to their ages. There is certainly plenty of advice out there for 'regular' parents who are splitting up via organisations like Relate and Voices in the Middle, and yet for many of us, seeking help and support in this area remains a taboo, something you do as a last resort when things go wrong rather than a healthy, important part of the process. I can't help thinking that a more consistent use of expert advice and services, a clearly signposted pathway through separation and adjusting to a new story, would help make the transition from one family to two single parent families not only a lot easier for children but more empowering for single mothers. Knowing exactly what to say and how to say it best for your child's age makes you the beacon in the storm, not part of the collateral damage. In its communications, Gingerbread talks about single families that are 'led by women', rather than single mothers. We need more of this positive language around the topic, and we need to help single mothers feel like they really are leaders. Because they are; it's just that no one tells them this very often or gives them medals or colours for their achievements.

Obviously, single mothers need more money. The financial situation you find yourself in really does have a huge impact on the way your single parent experience goes and on your children's crucial formative years. Again, solo mums tend to be in a better financial position and can often afford to live above the breadline. Following their lead on this hardly needs recommending. But not all single mothers get to achieve financial independence and security before they have children, and this is not something that they should be punished for, especially in a system that still favours the working hours and lifestyles of men and fathers. And simply making welfare more difficult for them to access will not magically send all those lazy, scrounging single mothers back to work, since they do genuinely have children to look after – they're not making them up.

As Susan Golombok's research at Cambridge concluded:

> Growing up with a divorced single mother does not in itself appear to be harmful. Instead it's the experiences that often go with single motherhood that cause the problems. One key factor is the drop in income experienced by many mothers following divorce, and that can be hard if not carefully managed.[42]

I've been awed by the work ethic and the grit and the ingenuity of all the single mothers I've talked to, all of them Amazons and not one of whom is enjoying a benefits lifestyle, since there is really nothing there to enjoy. What might the world look like if we back single mothers and their children, support them with the tax breaks, give them the deals, and reward their choices and hard work in the way we do married people? Help them get back to education and work, stop allowing non-paying parents to get away with it? I can't help thinking that society is missing a trick by trying so hard to keep all these fierce, resourceful and kind women down. And until we rid our culture and its biased systems of the misogyny and discrimination that affect all women, single or not, mothers or not, then we have still got even more work to do.

I remain absolutely fascinated by the Women's Day Off that happened in Iceland in 1975, the year I was born. On 24th October that year, 90 per cent of women in the country decided to demonstrate just how important they were by going on strike. Two hundred and twenty thousand women downed tools and marched while the men looked after the children and couldn't go to work. Sausages – easy to cook and a children's favourite – sold out across the land that day. And five years later, Iceland elected Vigdis Finnbogadottir – a divorced single mother and creative director of the Reykjavik Theatre Company – as their president. I

---

42 Susan Golombok (2020) *We Are Family: What Really Matters for Parents and Children.* London: Scribe.

like to wonder what would happen today, if all the single mothers went on strike. Can we all do that one day? Please?

But changing the world is a big ask, and single mums are busy raising their awesome children. Children who are not deprived or unloved, lacking because they only have one parent or confused because they have four, badly behaved or somehow behind in their cognitive development, but who are in fact adored, listened to, valued, nurtured and exceptionally secure in their relationships, not only with their mums, but with all of the many other people who wrap around them with love.

It is these children – who are being raised without blinkers, in the story of their own families' fairytales – who will ultimately change the way we think about single mothers and the fine human beings they raise. I hope that the time will come when no one tells them they're sorry, or asks when their father left or remarks on the situation at all. And although currently she swears she'll never have children, if my daughter says she wants to be a single mum when she grows up, I'll support her all the way. There's no shame in it, after all.

A LETTER FROM SARAH

Hello!

Thank you so much for reading this far. I really appreciate it and I hope this book has given you some food for thought, whether you're already a single mum or you're thinking of becoming one in the future (to which I say: do it!).

My publishers at Thread are all about inspiring memoirs and incredible stories, so if you are keen on reading more of this sort of thing, do sign up at the following link. Your email address will never be shared, and you can unsubscribe at any time.

www.thread-books.com/sign-up

Lots of people have asked me why this book isn't also about single dads and single fatherhood. One of the main reasons that it's not is that single fathers tend to assimilate themselves with new families more quickly and more often than single mothers, so while there are single dads around, they're often not around for long. And as men, they don't always come up against the same kinds of challenges, financial and social, that women do. So, on one level, this book isn't about them simply because as a demographic they're just not that meaty. Sorry, single dads.

But the other reason is that this is just my take on things. As I wrote this book, I was constantly reminded of the infinite number of ways there are to experience single parenthood. From an accidental one-night stand to a messy separation, from an untimely death to a long and difficult fertility journey. Families who embrace and accept single mothers, others who reject and vilify them. Big, fat divorce settlements and lives lived on the breadline.

As a trainee journalist I was taught to always 'dig where you stand' and that is what I have done. This book is about my experiences, and while I have tried to consider my story within the context of the bigger picture, the truth is that the picture is way too big for one lens. So this is my truth. One I consider to be exceptionally fortunate. Others will undoubtedly have different things to say about single motherhood. I hope more of all of our stories will be heard in the future.

I've shared details of some of the most useful resources that are available to single mothers at the bottom of this letter. I confess that when I started out, I felt a bit chippy about the fact that single parents had a charity like Gingerbread. I didn't see why we needed one. Coming out the other side of this project, I see how vitally important Gingerbread's work is and I would urge everyone to support this organisation if you can. Victoria Benson talks about the way in which single parents are so often overlooked in government and policymaking; it's not so much an intentional discrimination as a kind of institutionalised carelessness. But when you consider that one in four of us is now a single parent – one in three in the US – it means that if it's not actually you, it's probably your sister or your friend, who is handling — likely with much more dignity and polite silence than me – the unfairness of the single mother's lot. Anything you can do to support Gingerbread's work will be a leg-up for all of us.

One last thing! If you have enjoyed reading this book, I would be really grateful if you could leave a review. And you can always get in touch with me via Instagram (@mssarahgracet) or my website, sarahgthompson.com. I would genuinely be delighted to hear from you!

Again, thank you so much for reading this book. Here's to all the single mothers out there. As my daughter says: yes queens, slay!

Sarah

USEFUL SOURCES OF INFORMATION AND SUPPORT FOR SINGLE MOTHERS

Gingerbread
The single parent charity
www.gingerbread.org.uk

The Donor Conception Network
Support and advice for donor-conceived families
www.dcnetwork.org

Barnardo's
If you're thinking of adopting as a single parent
www.barnardos.org.uk

Child Maintenance Service
For information and advice on child maintenance
https://childmaintenanceservice.direct.gov.uk

StepChange
Free expert debt advice
www.stepchange.org

Citizens Advice
Advice on everything from benefits and housing to rights and employment
www.citizensadvice.org.uk

Relate
Relationship advice and counselling for families
www.relate.org.uk

Mind
If you are worried about your mental health
www.mind.org.uk

Voices in the Middle
A great resource for communicating with teenagers
www.voicesinthemiddle.com

Women's Aid
If you are experiencing domestic abuse
www.womensaid.org.uk

Shelter
For advice on housing
www.shelter.org.uk

Beauty Banks
If you are experiencing hygiene poverty
www.beautybanks.org.uk

The Trussell Trust
Find your nearest food bank
www.trusselltrust.org

ACKNOWLEDGEMENTS

Biggest of thankyous to my brilliant agent and solo mum supreme, Rowan Lawton at the Soho Agency. You really did save me, and this book. Thank you from the bottom of my heart. And to Claire Bord at Thread, for putting your faith in me, being so patient with me and sending reassuring messages of 'IT'S NOT RUBBISH' exactly when I needed to hear them. Thank you also to Myrto Kalavrezou and all the other lovely people at Thread.

Thank you to my incredible mum, Thelma, and my sisters, Peta and Jane, for all of your love, support and wisdom. Thank you doesn't really cover it. I couldn't do any of it without you. We love you all.

To my brilliant friends Debs, Jess, Anna and Lisa, all the very finest of women(extra special thanks to Debs for all the dog walks, he definitely loves you more than me now). And all the members of the world's best WhatsApp group: Chubby Googlebox – you have all been my extended family and source of the very best medicine for so many years. And thanks to all of the other friends and single mothers who gave me their time and insights while I was writing this book. Keep on truckin', all of you.

Thank you to Tom, without whom I would never have had the children or anyone to get divorced from. We didn't get everything right, but we made good kids. I know you are as proud as I am of them both. And sorry about writing this book; I know it's not the book every ex-husband dreams his ex-wife will write. I always did like to make a big fuss, right?

And finally to my children, Stanley and Betty. I love you and I love our little family, with our dog Louie, King of the Sausage People, and our cat Daphne, the evil killer queen. Thank you for looking after yourselves while I wrote a book about looking after you. I promise to be more normal now. Love you both always, Mum x

Made in the USA
Monee, IL
06 May 2022

95982405R00114